Up & Running Ser
from SYBEX

Computer users are not all alike.
Neither are SYBEX books.

We know our customers have a variety of needs. They've told us so. And because we've listened, we've developed several distinct types of books to meet the needs of each of our customers. What are you looking for in computer help?

If you're looking for the basics, try the **ABC's** series. You'll find short, unintimidating tutorials and helpful illustrations. For a more visual approach, select **Teach Yourself**, featuring screen-by-screen illustrations of how to use your latest software purchase.

Mastering and **Understanding** titles offer you a step-by-step introduction, plus an in-depth examination of intermediate-level features, to use as you progress.

Our **Up & Running** series is designed for computer-literate consumers who want a no-nonsense overview of new programs. Just 20 basic lessons, and you're on your way.

We also publish two types of reference books. Our **Instant References** provide quick access to each of a program's commands and functions. SYBEX **Encyclopedias** provide a *comprehensive reference* and explanation of all of the commands, features and functions of the subject software.

Sometimes a subject requires a special treatment that our standard series doesn't provide. So you'll find we have titles like **Advanced Techniques, Handbooks, Tips & Tricks**, and others that are specifically tailored to satisfy a unique need.

We carefully select our authors for their in-depth understanding of the software they're writing about, as well as their ability to write clearly and communicate effectively. Each manuscript is thoroughly reviewed by our technical staff to ensure its complete accuracy. Our production department makes sure it's easy to use. All of this adds up to the highest quality books available, consistently appearing on best seller charts worldwide.

You'll find SYBEX publishes a variety of books on every popular software package. Looking for computer help? Help Yourself to SYBEX.

For a complete catalog of our publications:

SYBEX Inc.
2021 Challenger Drive, Alameda, CA 94501
Tel: (415) 523-8233/(800) 227-2346 Telex: 336311
SYBEX Fax: (415) 523-2373

Up & Running
with DR DOS™ 5.0

Joerg Schieb

SYBEX ®

San Francisco • Paris • Düsseldorf • Soest

Acquisitions Editor: David Clark
Series Editor: Joanne Cuthbertson
Copy Editor: Brendan Fletcher
Technical Editor: Dan Tauber
Word Processors: Ann Dunn, Lisa Mitchell
Book Designer: Elke Hermanowski
Icon Designer: Helen Bruno
Screen Graphics: Cuong Le, Delia Brown
Desktop Production Artists: Helen Bruno, Claudia Smelser
Proofreaders: Lisa Haden, Hilda van Genderen
Indexer: Ted Laux
Cover Designer: Archer Design

SYBEX
Up & Running Books

The Up & Running series of books from SYBEX has been developed for committed, eager PC users who would like to become familiar with a wide variety of programs and operations as quickly as possible. We assume that you are comfortable with your PC and that you know the basic functions of word processing, spreadsheets, and database management. With this background, Up & Running books will show you in 20 steps what particular products can do and how to use them.

Who this book is for

Up & Running books are designed to save you time and money. First, you can avoid purchase mistakes by previewing products before you buy them—exploring their features, strengths, and limitations. Second, once you decide to purchase a product, you can learn its basics quickly by following the 20 steps—even if you are a beginner.

What this book provides

The first step usually covers software installation in relation to hardware requirements. You'll learn whether the program can operate with your available hardware as well as various methods for starting the program. The second step often introduces the program's user interface. The remaining 18 steps demonstrate the program's basic functions, using examples and short descriptions.

Contents and structure

 A clock shows the amount of time you can expect to spend at your computer for each step. Naturally, you'll need much less time if you only read through the step rather than complete it at your computer.

Special symbols and notes

You can also focus on particular points by scanning the short notes in the margins and locating the sections you are most interested in.

In addition, three symbols highlight particular sections of text:

The Action symbol highlights important steps that you will carry out.

The Tip symbol indicates a practical hint or special technique.

The Warning symbol alerts you to a potential problem and suggestions for avoiding it.

We have structured the Up & Running books so that the busy user spends little time studying documentation and is not burdened with unnecessary text. An Up & Running book cannot, of course, replace a lengthier book that contains advanced applications. However, you will get the information you need to put the program to practical use and to learn its basic functions in the shortest possible time.

We welcome your comments

SYBEX is very interested in your reactions to the Up & Running series. Your opinions and suggestions will help all of our readers, including yourself. Please send your comments to: SYBEX Editorial Department, 2021 Challenger Drive, Alameda, CA 94501.

Preface

DR DOS 5.0 replaces Digital Research's most successful DOS version thus far, DR DOS 3.41. The experience Digital Research has gathered with such operating systems as Concurrent DOS and CP/M has noticeably influenced DR DOS 5.0.

The new version is more compatible with MS-DOS, includes the JOIN command many users found to be lacking in the previous version, and provides an improved full-screen editor and a graphic user interface reminiscent of GEM. Another of the outstanding features of the new version allows you to free up to 620K of conventional memory for applications (provided extended memory is available). This is made possible by various clever additions to the system configuration.

Laptop manufacturers and users will be pleased to learn that DR DOS supports energy-saving measures, such as switching off a hard disk drive or a screen not in use, and permits data transmission via cable (FileLink).

There are a lot more surprises still in store for you, I promise! This book will help you get acquainted with the new operating system as quickly as possible.

Joerg Schieb

Table of Contents

Step 1

Installation

To install DR DOS, about all you need to do is make backups of your master disks, insert the appropriate disks into your drive, and follow the on-screen instructions provided at each step of installation. This step will guide you through this process and explain several variations on this general theme.

Preparing for Installation

You should make working copies of the disks provided with your DR DOS package to protect the originals against accidental damage. You will need four blank, formatted disks if you are using 5¼" disks, and three if you are using 3½" disks.

To make the copies, insert the Disk 1 into your A drive and type

```
DISKCOPY A: A:
```

DR DOS will then ask you to insert a blank disk. Do so, and follow all subsequent instructions. Repeat the process until you have copied all of your disks.

If you have two floppy disk drives of the same size, you can speed up the process by using the command

```
DISKCOPY A: B:
```

The INSTALL Program

Installing DR DOS is much the same whether you are installing to hard disk or to floppy disks. If you are installing to hard disk, you should keep in mind that your hard disk should be partitioned (normally your dealer or manufacturer will have done this). However, if it is not, the INSTALL program will detect this and will automatically partition it with a program called FDISK. If you are installing to floppies, your only special consideration is having 360K disks on hand.

When you are ready to install DR DOS, follow these steps:

1. Insert the Startup disk (#1) into drive A.

2. Press the Ctrl-Alt-Del keys simultaneously.

3. If you are using 360K disks, you will be prompted to insert the Install and Utilities disk (#2).

At this point, DR DOS will display a welcome screen including clear on-screen instructions. Follow these, selecting options as suits your needs. For the most part, you will find the instructions self-explanatory; however, the following options deserve special attention:

- Configuration size: If your hard disk already contains AUTOEXEC.BAT and CONFIG.SYS files, you can choose to have them ignored. (You should if you want a completely new installation of DR DOS 5.0.) After this you are asked to choose the default size of your DR DOS configuration. There are three choices here, each striking a different balance between application memory and DOS functionality. You should probably select the middle option as it is sufficient for most applications.

- ViewMAX: ViewMAX is the DR DOS graphic user interface, similar to the MS-DOS shell. If you want to have ViewMAX started automatically each time the system is booted, select the appropriate option.

- Command and system files: If you are installing DR DOS on a hard disk that was previously in use, the system suggests replacing all the command and system files on the hard disk with the new ones. You should accept this suggestion unless you have a good reason for not doing so (e.g., if you want to have two separate DOS versions on your disk).

Automatic configuration

After replacing (or not replacing) existing DOS files, you will see the screen in Figure 1.1. You will be asked whether you want the rest of the installation to be performed automatically, in which case all default configurations will be accepted, or whether you want to work through the configuration step by step. If you are not familiar with operating systems, it is wiser to accept the installation program's default settings. If, on the other hand, you are an experienced user, you might prefer to proceed through the configuration step by step (see "Configuring with SETUP" below).

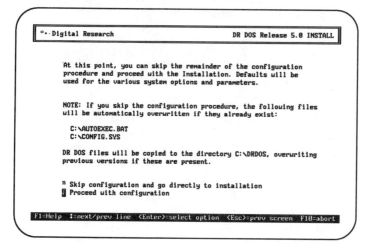

```
°··Digital Research                    DR DOS Release 5.0 INSTALL

        At this point, you can skip the remainder of the configuration
        procedure and proceed with the Installation. Defaults will be
        used for the various system options and parameters.

        NOTE: If you skip the configuration procedure, the following files
        will be automatically overwritten if they already exist:

           C:\AUTOEXEC.BAT
           C:\CONFIG.SYS

        DR DOS files will be copied to the directory C:\DRDOS, overwriting
        previous versions if these are present.

        ⁿ Skip configuration and go directly to installation
        ▌ Proceed with configuration

     F1=Help  ↕=next/prev line  <Enter>=select option  <Esc>=prev screen  F10=abort
```

Figure 1.1: Automatic installation vs. step-by-step configuration

Should you decide on automatic installation, all the command and system files will be copied into the \DRDOS directory that is created. At this point, the system prompts you to insert the appropriate system disk. The two system files, AUTOEXEC.BAT and CONFIG.SYS, are created automatically and can be displayed and edited at any time in the future by using the SETUP program.

AUTO-EXEC.BAT and CONFIG.-SYS

Once the installation is complete, reboot the computer by pressing Ctrl-Alt-Del.

Configuring with SETUP

If you become dissatisfied at any time with your default settings, you can change these through a DR DOS program called SETUP.

Although many users will never need to change any default settings, some will find the following options (and others) essential:

- You can define the directory names for the APPEND search path (the path for data files). In addition, the search path for command files may be expanded. It is a good idea to define your most frequently used directories here.

- Enabling the HISTORY command lets you edit the command line easily. (See Step 3.) Although this option can save you time in editing, its default setting is off as it has the effect of slowing down your system.

- If you have a 386 or better CPU, you should turn on the 80386 Memory Support (EMM386.SYS) and Relocate DR DOS Data Areas and Device Drivers options (see Figure 1.2). This will increase the amount of memory available to application programs that you run from DR DOS.

When you have finished selecting configuration options, you will see the screen in Figure 1.3. When you press Enter, SETUP will regenerate the system files and you will be finished.

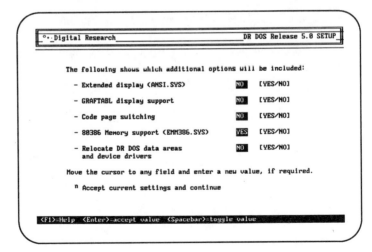

Figure 1.2: Some configuration options

```
┌─────────────────────────────────────────────────────────────────┐
│ °·.Digital Research_____DR DOS Release 5.0 SETUP │
│                                                                   │
│    This concludes the configuration procedure.                    │
│                                                                   │
│    To review or change any of your choices, you can backtrack     │
│    through the configuration screens using the <Esc> key.         │
│                                                                   │
│    The Setup Program will now update your DR DOS system.          │
│                                                                   │
│                                                                   │
│    ▌ Press <Enter> to continue.                                   │
│                                                                   │
│                                                                   │
│ <Enter>=select option  <Esc>=prev screen  <F10>=abort             │
└─────────────────────────────────────────────────────────────────┘
```

Figure 1.3: Configuration is complete

Step 2

User Interface

This step introduces you to ViewMAX, the DR DOS 5.0 graphic user interface. ViewMAX includes many of the features—icons, pull-down menus, dialog boxes, and more—that have made graphic environments famous for their ease of use. And while ViewMAX is designed to be navigated with a mouse, it can, unlike many graphic interfaces, be navigated almost as comfortably through the keyboard.

Starting ViewMAX

As discussed in Step 1, you can instruct DR DOS to load View-MAX automatically each time you start your computer. If, for some reason, you did not do so, you can start ViewMAX in one of two ways.

- If you have a hard disk, type **VIEWMAX** at the command prompt and press Enter.

- If you are using floppies, insert the VIEWMAX disk in drive A, type **VIEWMAX,** and press Enter.

The ViewMAX Screen

Once you have successfully started ViewMAX, it will display a screen divided into two windows, as shown in Figure 2.1. These windows, each of which can display the contents of a directory or a list of drives, are the means by which you select and otherwise manipulate your applications, files, and directories. Only one window (the one with the highlighted title bar) is active at any given time.

You can move between the two windows by rolling the mouse or, if you're using the keyboard, by pressing the Tab key. If you click on the resizing box in the upper right corner of a window, the window will be expanded to fill the whole screen. Clicking on it again will reduce the window to its original size. The close box backs

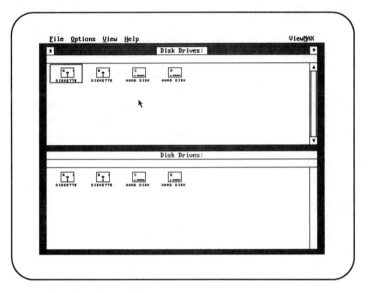

Figure 2.1: The ViewMAX screen

you up one level in the directory tree. If C:\DATA\JUNK is displayed, the first click on the close box will take you to C:\DATA, the second click brings you to C:\, and the third will display the list of disk drives. You can close the window by pressing Alt-F4.

A gray rectangle indicates the drive, directory, or file currently active. You can move from icon to icon by moving the mouse pointer or by pressing the appropriate arrow keys. If you want to change drives or directories, simply move the gray rectangle to the desired icon and either press Enter or double-click with the mouse.

Scroll bar

When a window contains more icons than can be viewed at any one time, you can use the *scroll bar* (if you are using a mouse) to move through the window line by line. Click on one of the scroll arrows at the top or bottom of the scroll bar to move in the direction desired. Clicking once will move the cursor one line in the indicated direction; holding down on the button will allow you to scroll through the list. If the window contains a very long list, you can drag the slider—the white box within the scroll bar—to move even more rapidly.

If you are using a keyboard, you can achieve an effect similar to the scroll bar's with the PgUp and PgDn keys.

Pull-down Menus

If you look back to Figure 2.1, you will see a number of options arranged horizontally along the menu bar. These are the titles of ViewMAX's *pull-down menus,* which list the various commands you can use within ViewMAX.

If you are using a mouse, you can pull down a menu by positioning the mouse pointer on the menu title. You don't have to press the left mouse button as you must in many other graphic user interfaces.

Mouse

If you're working with the keyboard, you pull down menus by pressing the Alt key in conjunction with the letter key for the underlined letter in the menu title. For example, you would type Alt-F for the File menu, Alt-H for Help, and so on. Once you have pulled down one menu, you can move between the menu items and between other pull-down menus with the arrow keys. Press Esc to return the window.

Keyboard

To select a menu item, click on it with the left mouse button or press Enter. You can also activate a menu item by pressing the key of the underlined letter in the item name. Whatever method you choose, the relevant menu item will be immediately activated.

Some commands cannot be chosen if they are not relevant to what you are doing at the time: these display in gray. The highlight cannot be positioned on commands that are not available.

Dialog Boxes

If you select a pull-down menu item that ends with an ellipsis, a dialog box will appear on your screen. Figure 2.2 shows a typical dialog box. If you are using the keyboard, you can move between fields using the Tab key. If you are using a mouse, you can, of course, move freely within the dialog box. Either way, a gray rectangle indicates the current field.

You can confirm a data entry field by pressing the Spacebar. Enter confirms all the entries in the window. You can change individual options and activate the buttons by clicking on them with the mouse or, if you are using the keyboard, by moving the cursor to the desired option and pressing Enter.

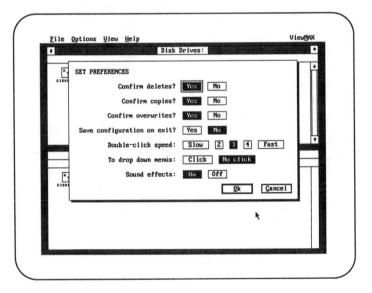

Figure 2.2: The Option Preferences dialog box

Displaying the Directory Structure

ViewMAX can illustrate the directory structure of a drive in a graphic "tree structure" display (see Figure 2.3). When you select the Tree option in the View menu, ViewMAX will read the appropriate drive and display its tree structure on your screen. You can select individual directories from the tree structure using the

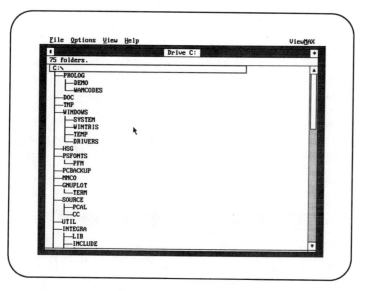

Figure 2.3: The tree structure of a drive in ViewMAX

mouse or the cursor keys and Enter. If you prefer text display, the View menu's Text option will display a list of file names instead of the icons.

Selecting Files

For some operations, you will want to highlight groups of files. Once the files are highlighted, you can perform a command, such as copying or moving, on the group. If you're using a keyboard, you can select and deselect a file using the Spacebar. If you are using a mouse, this operation is a little more cumbersome—when you click on a file or directory, it will be activated but previously selected ones will automatically be deselected. In order to select a group of files with the mouse, you need to hold the Shift key down while you point and click on each file to be selected.

There is a simpler way of selecting a whole group of files with the mouse: press and hold down the mouse button while you move

the mouse (a procedure referred to as *dragging*). A rectangle will
appear on the screen, as shown in Figure 2.4. This rectangle,
known in ViewMAX as a "rubber rectangle," expands or contracts
as you move the mouse pointer. All files and directories within the
rubber rectangle are selected as soon as you release the mouse
button.

Having selected the group of files you want, you can now select
a menu item such as File Copy and process the entire group in a
single operation.

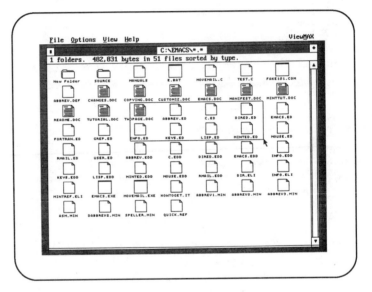

Figure 2.4: Selecting a group of files with the mouse

Step 3

Command Line

DR DOS provides a traditional command line in addition to the graphic user interface. Every time you access the DR DOS command level, the *system prompt* appears, signaling readiness to accept input. The prompt consists of the current drive letter followed by a greater-than sign. The name of the default directory is often included as well, as in the second and third examples below:

```
A>
C:\DOS>
D:\WP\TEXT>
```

A flashing cursor indicates your current position in the command line. You enter commands through the keyboard.

Standard Editing Functions

Many of the function keys can be used to expedite command entry. Table 3.1 summarizes the standard functions available for entering instructions at the command line.

Key	Function
Enter	Ends the current command line and causes DR DOS to execute the command.
F1	Transfers the next character from the DOS buffer and outputs it into the command line.
F2n	Transfers all characters up to the first appearance of the specified character (*n*) from the DOS buffer and outputs them into the command line. *n* itself is not copied.

Table 3.1: Standard assignment of the function keys at the system prompt

Key	Function
F3	Transfers all characters after the current position from the DOS buffer and outputs them.
F4n	Skips over the characters in the DOS buffer up to the first appearance of the character *n*. The internal pointer in the DOS buffer is on *n*.
F5	Copies the current line into the DOS buffer.
F6	Generates an end-of-file mark (EOF). This character can also be generated with Ctrl-Z.
F7	Corresponds to the key combination Ctrl-@.
Ins	Toggles between insert and overwrite mode.
Del	Erases the character the cursor is on.
Esc	Cancels the current command line. If HISTORY is active, the cursor appears at the start of the command line. If HISTORY is inactive, a backslash (\) appears at the end of the command line and the cursor moves to the next line.
Alt*nnn*	Creates the character with ASCII code *nnn*. The code must be entered on the number pad.
Backspace	The previous character is deleted and the cursor moves one space to the left.
PrtScr	Prints the current screen.

Table 3.1: Standard assignment of the function keys at the system prompt (continued)

Extended Editing Functions

Buffers

In Step 1, you learned that HISTORY gives you access to extended editing facilities. It is HISTORY's task to store previously entered command lines in a separate buffer and to recall these if necessary. HISTORY creates two buffers in your computer's memory for this purpose. These buffers can be between 128 and 4096 bytes in size and are specified in the CONFIG.SYS file. The larger the buffers, the more command lines can be stored. Two internal buffers are available, one for DR DOS's command lines and another for input to applications.

You can work through the list of command lines chronologically using the ↑ and ↓ keys. The ↑ key scrolls through the list of command lines starting from the end; ↓ scrolls from the beginning. When you reach the end of the list, you are automatically returned to the beginning. Each command line is copied into the current DOS buffer where it may be modified or confirmed immediately.

In addition, you can use the ← and → keys to edit the current command line. These keys allow you to move the cursor freely within the command line without deleting characters. In other words, you can neglect the more complicated method of editing command lines using the function keys.

Editing the current command line

When the HISTORY option is active, the standard keystrokes for editing shown in Table 3.1 are supplemented by those shown in Table 3.2.

Key	*Function*
← or Ctrl-S	Cursor is moved one character to the left in the current command line.
→ or Ctrl-D	Cursor is moved one character to the right in the current command line.
↑ or Ctrl-E	Loads the previous command line into the DOS buffer.
↓ or Ctrl-X	Loads the following command line into the DOS buffer.
Ctrl-A	Moves the cursor one word left.
Ctrl-F	Moves the cursor one word right.

Table 3.2: HISTORY's extended editing functions

Key	Function
Home	Moves the cursor to the beginning of the line.
End	Moves the cursor to the end of the line.
Ctrl-T	Deletes from the cursor to the end of the word.
Ctrl-Y	Deletes the entire command line.
Ctrl-B	Deletes all the characters before the cursor.
Ctrl-K	Deletes all the characters to the end of a line.
Ctrl-_	Turns command line search mode on and off. When search mode is on, DR DOS searches for the first command line that matches the characters you have typed.
Ctrl-R	DR DOS searches for and displays the first command line that matches the characters typed.

Table 3.2: HISTORY's extended editing functions (continued)

Entering a Command Line

Uppercase versus lowercase

How you enter a command line in DR DOS is basically the same whether or not HISTORY is active. DOS commands may be entered in uppercase or lowercase letters. If file names are to follow a command or an application name, these must be separated from the command itself by at least one blank. A list of file names must also be separated by at least one blank. Options may be listed without spaces, as shown below:

```
DIR *.TXT /W/P
```

The *.TXT file name is separated from the DOS command by a blank, whereas it is not necessary to separate the two options from each other or from the file name.

A command line that you have executed with Enter may, of course, be edited at any time in the future, as described above. Identical or similar command lines that are to be executed repeatedly may be retrieved using F3 and then edited if necessary.

Please note the search path defined by PATH. The commands you invoke can be executed only if DR DOS finds the search path in the default directory or in a directory defined in the search path (see Step 5). It is also possible to specify the drive and the directory where the command file is located. For example, if your word processor (we'll say you use WordPerfect) is not in the search path, you would start the application with the following command:

```
\WP\WP SAMPLE.TXT
```

Using HISTORY's Features

The following examples should help you more fully understand HISTORY's features. Suppose, for example, you type the following command by mistake:

```
ETASE *.BAK
```

The command should, of course, be ERASE, and an appropriate error message will duly be displayed. If HISTORY is not active, you can correct your mistake as follows:

1. Press F1 to copy the first character, *E.*

2. Type **R** to replace the wrong character, *T.*

3. Press F3 to copy the rest of the old command into the command line.

4. Press Enter to confirm the corrected command line.

If, however, HISTORY is active, the correction is much simpler and more convenient. (However, you still have the option of using the longer method if you feel more comfortable with it.) You can proceed like this:

1. Press ↑ to transfer the last command line into the editor.

2. Press Home to place the cursor on the first character.

3. Press ↓ to place the cursor on the second character.

4. Type **R** to replace the wrong character, *T.*

5. Press Enter to confirm the corrected command line.

If your correction mainly entails inserting or deleting characters, it is much more convenient to use HISTORY than to work with the function keys.

Now let's examine a special search mode that HISTORY offers. Type in the following four commands:

```
CLS
DIR *.* /W/P
VERIFY ON
VOL C:
```

Now hold down the Shift key and press Ctrl-_. This activates the special search mode. Type **D**, and the DIR command, which is the second command you entered, will appear on the screen. This is because HISTORY has searched for the first command in the buffer containing a match for the character you entered, and the DIR command fits the bill. However, if you type **O**, the command line will be reduced to DO as there is no matching character in the buffer. Let's erase DO, and try another example: Type **V**, and the VERIFY command will be displayed. If you then type **O**, VERIFY will be replaced by VOL, as two characters can now be matched. HISTORY displays the first command line in the internal buffer that matches all the characters you have typed so far.

Internal and External Commands

Internal commands

DOS makes a fundamental distinction between internal and external commands. *Internal commands* (also known as resident commands) are always available as they are loaded into the computer's conventional memory when DOS boots up. These commands are generally small but vital commands such as CLS, COPY, or DIR.

With *external commands,* the appropriate command file must be loaded from the disk before the command can be executed. Every application program is therefore an external command. If the command file is not available, the command cannot be executed.

External commands

External commands can be performed only when they are located in the default directory or a search path defined by PATH. Alternatively, you can execute external commands by specifying the drive and directory where the relevant command file is located before the command.

Table 3.3 lists all internal and external DR DOS commands. You will learn about the functions of many of these commands as you continue to work through this book. For more information, refer to the *DR DOS 5.0 User Guide.*

Internal Commands	External Commands
@	APPEND
:<label>	ATTRIB
ASSIGN	BACKUP
BREAK	CACHE
CALL	CHKDSK
CHCP	COMMAND
CHDIR|CD	COMP
CLS	CURSOR
COPY	DISKCOMP
CTTY	DISKCOPY

Table 3.3: Internal and external commands

Internal Commands	External Commands
DATE	EDITOR
DEL|ERA|ERASE	EXE2BIN
DELQ|ERAQ	FASTOPEN
DIR	FDISK
ECHO	FILELINK
EXIT	FIND
FOR	FORMAT
GOTO	GRAFTABL
HILOAD	GRAPHICS
IF	JOIN
MKDIR|MD	KEYB
MORE	LABEL
PATH	MEM
PAUSE	MODE
PROMPT	NLSFUNC
REM	PASSWORD
RENAME|REN	PRINT
RMDIR|RD	RECOVER
SET	REPLACE
SHIFT	RESTORE
SUBST	SETUP
TIME	SHARE
TYPE	SID
VER	SORT

Table 3.3: Internal and external commands (continued)

Internal Commands	External Commands
VERIFY	SYS
VOL	TOUCH
	TREE
	XCOPY
	XDEL
	XDIR

Table 3.3: Internal and external commands (continued)

The Help Function

Every external DR DOS command has associated help text you can display on the screen at any time. The help text lists the command's exact syntax, valid parameters, possible options and a brief description of the command itself. Such help text is not available for internal commands, as it would take up an excessive amount of memory.

Use the /H option to display a command's help text. For example, the help text of the ATTRIB command would be displayed by the following command:

```
ATTRIB /H
```

If you press Ctrl-P before issuing the help text command, the help text is also sent to the printer. To print all the available help pages, press Ctrl-P and issue the following command:

```
CD \DRDOS
FOR %A IN (*.EXE *.COM) DO %A /H
```

If your working directory is called \DOS instead of \DRDOS, modify the command accordingly.

With few exceptions, all floppy disks and hard disks need to be formatted before DR DOS can use them. (Some manufacturers provide disks that are already formatted.) To format a floppy disk, you use the DR DOS FORMAT command. (Formatting a hard disk is a more involved task; see Step 17 for details.)

The formatting process structures the disk in *tracks* and *sectors*. This means that formatting irrevocably erases everything stored on a floppy or hard disk; you must take care not to format a disk containing important files. Before formatting, you should make sure that you have a suitable disk drive and good quality disks.

Tracks and sectors

To format a disk, give the FORMAT command and specify the drive containing the disk to be formatted, as below:

FORMAT D:

In its simplest form, the FORMAT command formats both sides of the entire disk. You can modify the way in which a disk is formatted by adding parameters to the command. The full complement of parameters and their functions is summarized in Table 4.1.

Option	Effect
/H	Displays help text.
/1	Formats only one side of a disk (360K disks only).
/4	Formats a disk with 9 instead of 15 or 18 sectors per track (360K disks in 1.2Mb disk drives only).
/8	Formats 9 sectors per track but uses only 8.
/B	Reserves space for copying the two DOS system files (5¼" only).
/F:*nnn*	Formats the disk in the capacity specified in Kbytes.

Table 4.1: The FORMAT command's options

Option	Effect
/N:*xx*	Defines the number of sectors per track (8, 9, 15 or 18).
/S	Copies the two hidden system files and the COMMAND.COM file onto the target disk.
/T:*yy*	Sets the number of tracks (40 or 80).
/V	Enables you to enter a volume label for the disk or hard disk after formatting.

Table 4.1: The FORMAT command's options (continued)

Disk Density and Disk Size

A disk's storage capacity is determined by the number of tracks and sectors that can be accommodated on it. This in turn depends on the maximum storage density a disk can achieve. There are two disk densities, double density and high density. More information can be stored in the same space on a high density disk. Table 4.2 shows the different disk formats DR DOS supports.

Disk	Drive	Capacity	Tracks	Sectors tpi
5¼" SS/DD	160K	40	8	48
5¼" SS/DD	180K	40	9	48
5¼" DS/DD	320K	40	8	48
5¼" DS/DD	360K	40	9	48
5¼" DS/HD	1.2Mb	80	15	96
3½" DS/DD	720K	80	9	135
3½" DS/HD	1.44Mb	80	18	135

Table 4.2: Disk formats supported by DR DOS

When you are formatting a disk drive, FORMAT generally selects the appropriate format automatically unless you have specified options to be applied. The format that FORMAT automatically selects depends on the disk drive you have. It will always use the disk format with the maximum storage capacity. For example, on an AT with a 5¼" high-capacity drive, the 1.2Mb format will be used unless you have explicitly specified a different format. If you only have one 360K disk drive in your PC, a disk inserted will be formatted with only 360K. The same applies to 3½" disk drives.

Maximum storage capacity

Disk formats

The four main types of disk formats are 360 and 720K, and 1.2 and 1.44Mb. If there is a reason why you don't want to use the maximum storage format (e.g., because you want to give the disk to a user whose computer cannot read this format, or because the disk you are using is not up to standard), you must specify appropriate options.

To format a 360K disk in a 1.2Mb disk drive, for example, use the /4 option:

FORMAT A: /4

To format a 720K disk in a 1.44Mb drive (3½"), use the /N and /T options:

FORMAT A: /N:9 /T:80

As simple as that is, it is even more convenient to use the /F: switch to specify the desired storage capacity of the target diskette in kilobytes, irrespective of the type of disk drive in use. A 720K disk, for example, would be formatted with the following command:

FORMAT A: /F:720

There are a total of seven different /F: switch formats you can use for formatting. These are listed in Table 4.3.

Storage Capacity	Option
160K	/F:160
180K	/F:180
320K	/F:320
360K	/F:360
720K	/F:720
1.2Mb	/F:1200
1.44Mb	/F:1440

Table 4.3: Formats supported by the /F: switch

Step 5

System Commands

DR DOS provides a set of commands whose function it is to run the system. The system date and time, for example, are important components of your system. If your computer is not equipped with a battery-backed clock, you will be prompted for the current date and time each time you start or reset your computer. DR DOS needs this data in order to record the current date and time whenever you create or modify a file, a procedure known as date-stamping. The date stamp enables you to see at a glance the last time a file was modified.

The Internal Calendar and Clock

Using the DATE command, you can display and if necessary amend the current system date. Type

DATE

and press Enter. DR DOS will display the following message:

```
Date: day dd-mm-yy
Enter date: (mm-dd-yy):
```

If you only want to consult the date and not change it, confirm it by pressing Enter. To enter a new date, adhere to the format shown above. Unless you have specified another country code in the CONFIG file, the American date format will be used. Invalid dates will be rejected and the following message displayed:

```
Invalid date specified
```

The system time can be displayed and set using the TIME command. Type

TIME

DATE

TIME

and press Enter. DR DOS will display the following:

```
Time: hh:mm:ss:xx
Enter time:
```

You can either confirm the displayed time by pressing Enter or set a new time. The new time you type in will be set when you press Enter. You may include seconds in the time if you wish.

If you don't need to check the system date and time to know that you want to change it, you can do so directly at the command line. Here are two examples:

```
DATE 6-8-1990
TIME 12:31
```

Clearing the Screen

CLS

The CLS command allows you to clear the screen at any time. The cursor then appears in the top left corner.

Which DR DOS Version Are You Using?

VER

The VER command indicates which version of DR DOS is currently in use. If you are working with version 5.0, typing

```
VER
```

results in the following message:

```
DR DOS Version 5.0
```

This feature is, of course, superfluous as long as you always work with the same computer. However, when you start a session at a new computer, it can be useful to find out which operating system version is installed so that you know which commands are available.

The DR DOS Search Path

When you instruct DR DOS to perform a command, it searches in the current directory for the matching command file unless you have explicitly specified a different directory. The same applies to data files. By using a *search path,* you can instruct DR DOS to search for a command or data file not found by a search of the current directory. DR DOS will search the directories in the search path in the order you list them.

The Search Path for Command Files

The PATH command sets a search path for command files. If DR DOS is not able to locate a command in the current directory, it searches each directory specified by PATH for the appropriate command file with one of the three possible extensions: .COM, .EXE or .BAT (in that order).

PATH

The individual directories must be separated by semicolons as in the example below:

```
PATH C:\DRDOS;D:\WP;C:\BATCHES;C:\123
```

The Search Path for Data Files

You can define a search path for data files using the APPEND command. As with command files, DR DOS searches through the specified directories if it does not find the specified file in the current directory. The syntax is identical to that of the PATH command:

APPEND

```
APPEND C:\DRDOS;C:\DATA;D:\TEXTS
```

To display the current search path, simply enter APPEND without parameters. APPEND may also be used with the options shown in Table 5.1.

Option	Effect
/X:[ON|OFF]	When this option is ON, the specified search path is also used as a search path for command files. The default setting is OFF.
/E:[ON|OFF]	The specified search path is also kept in the DOS environment (SET command). The default setting is OFF.
/PATH:[ON|OFF]	APPEND will not search the directories in the search path if a directory or drive is explicitly specified along with the filename (OFF). The default setting is ON.

Table 5.1: The APPEND command's options

The System Prompt

PROMPT

The default system prompt merely informs the user of the current default drive. With the aid of the PROMPT command, you can customize the prompt so that it contains more information. If, for example, you would like the current date and the system time to be displayed alongside the default drive, type

```
PROMPT It is $D, $T$H$H$H$_$p$g
It is Fri 8-06-1990, 22:58:23
C:\DRDOS>_
```

You see the result! In addition to ASCII character strings, you can use as many of the variables in Table 5.2 as you like, preceding each with a dollar sign. DR DOS replaces these by current values when displaying.

If you define a lengthy system prompt for which you don't have enough environment memory, DR DOS will give an error message telling you that the environment is full. Step 20 explains how you can go about setting up more environment memory during booting.

Code	Meaning
$B	Vertical bar (|)
$D	Current date
$E	Escape character
$G	Greater-than symbol (>)
$H	Deletes the character to the left of the cursor
$L	Less-than symbol (<)
$N	Default drive letter
$P	Current directory
$Q	Equals symbol (=)
$T	Current system time (Format: hh:mm:ss:tt)
$V	DR DOS version
$_	CR/LF; carriage return (new line)
$$	Dollar character ($)

Table 5.2: The PROMPT command's variables

Environment Memory

DR DOS and certain application programs keep variable strings in the DOS system environment. You can access this part of your computer's memory by using the SET command. If you type SET without adding parameters, the strings already in the environment will be displayed:

SET

```
SET
COMSPEC=C:\DRDOS\COMMAND.COM
OS=DRDOS
PROMPT=$P$G
PATH=C:\DRDOS;C:\WP
```

SET also lets you define your own variable strings or change existing ones. For example, you could define a search path as follows:

```
SET PATH=C:\DRDOS;C:\WP
```

To delete a variable string from the environment, simply type the name of the variable followed by an equals sign (=).

Running DR DOS on a Network

SHARE

If you want to operate your computer as part of a network, you must start the SHARE program. SHARE installs itself as a resident program and manages files accessed by different users at the same time. SHARE has to be loaded in addition to your network software. It lets you define how many file locks you want (*n* equals the number of locks):

```
SHARE [/L:n]
```

SHARE can be switched off at any time by the /X option.

Redirecting Output to and from Drives

There are two different commands in DR DOS that allow you to cause commands that would normally access a certain drive to access another drive or a subdirectory instead.

Reassigning One Drive as Another

ASSIGN

If an application program doesn't allow you to specify your choice of drive, you can use ASSIGN to redefine a drive letter. For example, to cause commands that would access drive A to access C instead, you would type the command

```
ASSIGN A=C
```

Use the /A option to check current assignments and no parameters at all to cancel all current statements.

You should only use ASSIGN if you really have to, since some programs ignore the ASSIGN statements. BACKUP, JOIN, LABEL, PRINT, RESTORE, and SUBST should never be used in connection with ASSIGN drives.

Reassigning a Drive as a Subdirectory

The SUBST command is much more convenient and powerful than the ASSIGN command. SUBST allows a virtual drive to represent an existing subdirectory. A virtual drive (G:) is created as follows:

SUBST

```
SUBST G: C:\DRDOS
```

You can now access the G drive. The C:\DRDOS directory will be the root directory of the new virtual drive. This method not only saves you typing time, it also solves the problem caused by programs that don't allow you to specify a directory. Up to 26 virtual drives may be created (A through Z).

```
SUBST
B: => C:\
G: => C:\DRDOS
H: => C:\DRDOS\BATCHES
```

Enter the SUBST command without parameters to display current substitutions. To remove a substitution, type the appropriate drive letter followed by the /D option:

```
SUBST G: /D
```

Connecting a Directory to a Drive

The JOIN command lets you connect a directory to a logical drive. This is useful when an application program does not offer a free choice of drive or you want to connect drives as if they were one large drive. The directory joined to the logical drive must be empty; that is, it must contain no files. The JOIN command was not available in the 3.41 version of DR DOS.

JOIN

You can connect the hard disks D and C by issuing the following command:

```
JOIN D: C:\DRIVED
```

When you execute this command, JOIN automatically creates a directory called \DRIVED. The D drive is no longer known to the system. Display the \DRIVED directory as follows:

```
DIR C:\DRIVED
```

As you see, the directory of the hard disk drive D is displayed. The information on free memory capacity refers to the C drive and not the D drive in this case.

If you invoke JOIN without parameters, DR DOS will display the drives currently connected. The /D parameter cancels the JOIN command, although it does not automatically remove the directory. This means that if you want the directory removed, you have to do it manually:

```
JOIN D: /D \DRIVED
```

Control Commands

DR DOS provides a set of commands that let you configure the system while working with it.

Interrupting During Disk Access

BREAK

The BREAK option allows you to stop a running program—even while disks are being accessed—by pressing Ctrl-Break or Ctrl-C. This is normally not permitted, but if you work with programs that access your disks and hard disks frequently and for lengthy periods, the ability to interrupt can be useful. To enable the BREAK option, type

```
BREAK ON
```

Verifying Data Written to the Disk

DR DOS can be instructed to verify the readability of written data, an important facility for ensuring data integrity. If you type

VERIFY ON

DR DOS checks after each sector is written whether it is readable. Both VERIFY and BREAK display the current system status if they are entered without parameters.

Defining the Standard Input/Output Device

The console, which is the screen and keyboard considered as a logical unit, is the default input/output device. Using CTTY, you can define another device as the default input/output device. The following example defines the serial port as the default:

CTTY

CTTY COM1

Information on Memory

Your computer's memory can be divided into conventional, extended, and expanded memory in several different ways, depending on the PC model you have. The MEM command displays information on your computer's current memory settings. Used on its own, MEM merely displays the current memory status. In conjunction with the options shown in Table 5.3, however, it can display more extensive information, such as the name of the device drivers installed, how conventional memory is being used, or a clear graphic display of memory status. Figure 5.1 shows the graphic display of memory accessed by the command

MEM

MEM /M

Parameter	Effect
/A	Displays all information.
/B	Shows areas of memory used.
/D	Shows device drivers.
/M	Shows the memory map.
/P	Displays information a screenful at a time.
/S	Displays the system structure.

Table 5.3: The MEM command's syntax and options

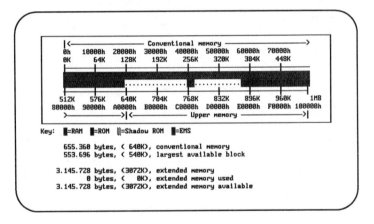

Figure 5.1: MEM provides information on the current memory settings

Leaving the Command Processor

EXIT

Certain applications allow you to access the DOS command line without leaving the application. The application can do this by loading a copy of the COMMAND.COM command processor. When you want to return to the application from which you temporarily accessed DOS, type

    EXIT

Copying Files

Anyone who works regularly with a PC knows that you often need to copy files and disks. DR DOS provides you with various utilities for performing these tasks.

Copying Files with COPY

The COPY command lets you copy individual files or whole groups of files, create files, and access peripherals. If a specific file is to be copied, enter the name of the source and the destination (drive, directory, or both). The following command copies the file SOURCE.TXT from the current directory to the \DEST directory on the C drive, where it retains the same file name:

```
COPY SOURCE.TXT C:\DEST
```

If you want the file to be renamed, you must specify the new name in the command line:

```
COPY SOURCE.TXT C:\DEST\NEWNAME.TXT
```

To copy several files at the same time, use the wildcard characters * and ?. For example, to copy all files with the .TXT extension, you would type:

Wildcard characters

```
COPY *.TXT C:\DEST
```

The COPY command also allows you to copy several files and merge these together into one destination file:

```
COPY A.TXT+B.TXT+C.TXT DEST.TXT
```

With COPY, you can also create a file at the keyboard:

```
COPY CON DEMO.TXT
These lines were typed on the keyboard.
Ctrl-Z
```

(Ctrl-Z is known as the end-of-file mark.)

Table 6.1 lists the options that can be used to modify the COPY command.

Option	Effect
/A	The file is treated like an ASCII (text) file, ending with the end-of-file mark. If /A is specified before the destination, the destination file will automatically receive an end-of-file mark.
/B	The file is not an ASCII file and ends with the actual end of the file. If /A is specified before the destination, the destination file will not contain an EOF character (Ctrl-Z).
/C	Asks for confirmation before copying each file.
/S	Copies system and hidden files.
/V	The accuracy of the destination file is checked after the copying process is finished.
/Z	Zeros the high bit of every byte in the destination file.

Table 6.1: The COPY command's options

Copying Easily with XCOPY

Any copying tasks COPY cannot perform can almost certainly be accomplished with XCOPY. XCOPY is an extended COPY command. If groups of files are to be copied, XCOPY loads as many as possible before starting to copy, which speeds up copying onto a disk. A special feature of XCOPY is that it can access subdirectories, whereas COPY can only copy a specified directory. If, for instance, you wanted to copy all the files on your hard disk with the extension .TXT onto a disk, you could accomplish this with the aid of the /S switch, as follows:

```
XCOPY C:\*.TXT A: /S
```

XCOPY will ensure that the directory structure on the hard disk is copied exactly onto the floppy disk. As with many commands,

you can tailor XCOPY to your needs with a variety of options.
These are shown in Table 6.2.

Option	Effect
/A	Copies only those files modified since the last BACKUP or XCOPY /M, whereby the archive attribute is not changed.
/D:*date*	Copies only files created or modified after the specified date.
/E	Creates a subdirectory at the destination even if this remains empty. Should be used only in conjunction with /S.
/H	Displays a help screen.
/M	Copies only those files changed since the last BACKUP or XCOPY /M. The archive attribute is reset.
/P	You are asked to confirm each file to be copied individually.
/R	Overwrites read-only files.
/S	XCOPY includes all the subdirectories at the source.
/V	Verifies accuracy of the copy at the destination.
/W	XCOPY waits for a disk to be inserted before starting to search for source files and again before copying, allowing you to change disks in the drive.

Table 6.2: The XCOPY command's options

If the @ character precedes the name of the source file, XCOPY
won't copy the file itself; however, it interprets the file names defined in the file and copies these. For example, if you copied the
file LIST.LST containing the files DEMO.TXT, \WP\WP.EXE,
and D:\DEMO\UTILITY\ALL.BAT, only the latter three files
would be copied to the destination. This switch can also be used in
conjunction with other switches.

*@ defines
file lists*

Copying a Complete Diskette

DISKCOPY

DR DOS also enables you to copy complete disks. The DISKCOPY command produces an identical copy of a disk. You can only copy a disk to one of the same size and format, that is, a 3½" disk to a 3½" one and a 5¼" one to a 5¼" one. You cannot use DISKCOPY to copy a hard disk. To copy a disk, type

```
DISKCOPY A: B:
```

If the destination disk is not appropriately formatted, DISKCOPY will format it during the copying process. If your computer only has one disk drive, you can still use DISKCOPY:

```
DISKCOPY A: A:
```

In this case, DISKCOPY prompts you to exchange the source and destination disks as necessary. How often you need to swap disks depends on the format of your disks and your computer's memory settings.

Updating Files

REPLACE

The REPLACE command is, in a sense, a copy command for up-dating files. It can be used to replace your out-of-date floppy disk files with your current hard disk file. You don't even need to explicitly define which files are to be copied; just supply the name of the directory containing the files. If the destination directory is empty, no files will be copied unless you use an appropriate option. Table 6.3 shows possible choices.

Option	Effect
/A	Copies only those files not already on the destination.
/H	Displays help text if /H is the first switch. Otherwise it serves to copy hidden or system files.

Table 6.3: The REPLACE command's options

Option	Effect
/M	Those files newly created or changed that do not already exist in the destination directory will be copied.
/P	Prompts you to confirm each file before copying.
/R	Read-only files on the destination will be replaced.
/S	Copies only those files that already exist on the destination.
/W	Allows disks to be changed before starting.
/U	Copies only those files that are older in the destination than in the source.

Table 6.3: The REPLACE command's options (continued)

Be careful never to confuse source and destination, as this could result in the wrong files being overwritten. First, define which files are to be copied, and then define where they are to be copied to. To replace all .TXT files on a disk with those on the hard disk, type

```
REPLACE \TEXTS\*.TXT A:
```

Even if, in this example, there were more .TXT files in the \TEXTS directory than on drive A, only those .TXT files already located on drive A would be copied. As with XCOPY, REPLACE allows you to specify a list of file names using @.

Copying the System Files

The SYS command can make a disk bootable by copying the COMMAND.COM, IBMBIO.COM, and IBMDOS.COM files to the disk. Note that the names of the system files have changed under DR DOS 5.0. IBMBIO.COM and IBMDOS.COM must be copied as in PC-DOS. In the case of DR DOS, though, both system files can be copied even if there are already files on the destination. The system files are always copied from the current drive

SYS

to the specified drive. If the hard disk is the default drive, you can copy the system files to a disk as follows (assuming the system files are on the hard disk):

```
SYS A:
```

Protecting Data

BACKUP

To make backup copies of your files, you use BACKUP. The advantage of BACKUP is that it can copy files larger than the storage space on the destination disk. BACKUP automatically numbers the required destination disks. Backup copies made with BACKUP must be restored using the RESTORE command before they can be used. The BACKUP command's syntax is as follows:

```
BACKUP source destination [options]
```

Table 6.4 shows the BACKUP command's options.

Option	Effect
/A	Causes data to be added to an existing backup.
/D:*date*	Copies only those files created or modified on or after the date specified.
/F	The destination disk is formatted before the files are copied if necessary.
/H	Displays help text.
/L:[*logfile*]	Creates a log file. Unless you specify a file name, the file will be called BACKUP.LOG.
/M	Causes all the files whose archive bit is set to be copied. The archive bit can be reset by a number of programs, including XCOPY, ATTRIB, and BACKUP, and other backup software such as FastBack.

Table 6.4: The BACKUP command's options

Option	Effect
/S	Includes subdirectories.
/T:*time*	Copies only those files created or modified since the specified time; can only be used in conjunction with /D.

Table 6.4: The BACKUP command's options (continued)

The files to be copied constitute the first parameter in the BACKUP command. You usually specify a drive or a directory as the destination. Unless you are using the /A switch, all the files at the destination will be deleted. To copy the complete hard disk C onto floppy disk, type

```
BACKUP C:\*.* A: /S
```

/S causes all associated subdirectories to be copied. It is also possible to copy only certain files. In the following example, only those .TXT files in the TEXTS subdirectory whose archive bit is set will be copied:

```
BACKUP D:\TEXTS\*.TXT A: /M
```

You should generally use disks that have already been formatted. Using the /F switch, you can instruct BACKUP to format unformatted disks before using them. Remember that the disks will be formatted with the maximum format of the drive. For example, a 360K format won't be used in a 1.2Mb drive.

Restoring Backup Copies

RESTORE restores backup files and directories produced with the BACKUP utility. RESTORE knows the numbering of the BACKUP disks and prompts you to insert each in turn. RESTORE basically copies files back to the source directory. A file from the \ALPHA directory can't, for example, be restored to \BETA. The RESTORE command's syntax is as follows:

RESTORE

```
RESTORE source destination [options]
```

Table 6.5 shows RESTORE's options:

Option	Effect
/A:*date*	Restores only those files created or modified after the specified date.
/B:*date*	Restores only those files created before on or before the specified date.
/E:*time*	Restores only those files created or modified before the specified time.
/H	Displays help text.
/M	Restores all files that have been created or modified since last backup.
/N	Restores only those files that do not exist on the destination.
/P	Prompts you for confirmation in the case of read-only and hidden files or when the destination file is more recent than the source file.
/R	Displays on the screen the names of all the files that would be restored without restoring them.
/S	Subdirectories are restored.
/T:*time*	Restores only those files created or modified after the time specified.

Table 6.5: The RESTORE command's options

If, for example, you want to copy all the .TXT files deleted since the last backup onto your hard disk, type

```
RESTORE A: C:\*.TXT /S /N
```

If you deleted some files dated before 8/1/90 and want to restore them, type the following:

```
RESTORE A: C:\*.* /S /A:8/1/1990
```

Verifying Copies

The COMP command is used to compare two files. COMP compares the files character by character and displays character
mismatches on the screen in the following format:

```
Offset xxxxh source=yyh  destination=zzh
```

COMP

The comparison is discontinued after ten located mismatches (this
number can be changed using the /M switch). COMP's syntax is
as follows:

```
COMP [file1 [file2]] [/A] [/M:n]
```

Table 6.6 shows the COMP command's options.

Option	Effect
/H	Displays help text.
/A	Displays the mismatches in ASCII format instead of the default hexadecimal format.
/M:*n*	Specifies the maximum number of mismatches before COMP terminates automatically.

Table 6.6: The COMP command's options

If you have only specified one file name, or none at all, COMP
prompts you to type in the file names on the keyboard. If the destination file name is identical to the source file name, it is only
necessary to define the appropriate drive or directory.

Comparing Disks

DISKCOMP enables you to compare two disks, provided, of
course, they have an identical format. To compare two disks, type

```
DISKCOMP A: B:
```

DISKCOMP

DISKCOMP can also work with only one drive, in which case
you specify the name of the drive twice. DISKCOMP prompts

you to swap disks as necessary:

```
DISKCOMP A: A:
```

DISKCOMP compares the disks sector by sector and will report an error if files are located in different places on the disks, even though the files are identical in content. Use the /V switch to check if all the sectors on a disk are usable:

```
DISKCOMP A: /V
```

In order to manage your files properly, you must delete some from time to time. DR DOS, unlike other DOS versions, provides a whole range of handy commands for deleting files.

DEL

DEL deletes an individual file or a group of files. Following deletion, a file can be retrieved with such programs as the Norton Utilities or PC Tools, provided you have not created new files or modified existing ones in the meantime. To delete a specific file, type

```
DEL \TEXTS\CERTAIN.TXT
```

To delete a group of files, use the wildcards * and ?. When you try to delete all the files in a directory, the following prompt will be displayed on the screen:

```
DEL \TEXTS\*.*
Are you sure (Y/N)?
```

DEL will delete all the files in the specified directory only if you type **Y**. If you don't specify files, but only a directory, DEL will assume you mean *.*.

If you use the /C switch, you have to confirm each individual file before it is deleted. The /S switch makes DEL delete hidden and system files.

Switches

ERA and ERASE

The ERA and ERASE commands have the same function as DEL. These commands are still in existence due only to their compatibility with CP/M (a precursor to MS-DOS).

DELQ and ERAQ

The DELQ and ERAQ commands are identical to the DEL command in combination with the /C switch. You will be prompted to confirm each file before it is erased.

XDEL

XDEL is the most convenient of all DR DOS 5.0's delete commands, although it is an external command. The command's syntax is suitably extensive:

```
XDEL [/H] [@]files [/D] [/N] [/O] [/P] [/R]
[/S]
```

Table 7.1 lists XDEL's options.

Option	Effect
@	A list of file names to be deleted is defined in the files file.
/H	Displays help text.
/D	Automatically deletes empty directories.
/N	Deletes all specified files without asking for confirmation.
/O	Overwrites the data in the deleted file so the file can never be recovered, even with PC Tools or the Norton Utilities.
/P	Prompts you before deleting each file.
/R	Deletes read-only files as well.
/S	The operation extends to subdirectories.

Table 7.1: The XDEL command's options

XDEL can be useful in solving some common problems. For example, it can be instructed to delete a directory if it becomes empty following the deletion of the files in it, so that you don't have to use the RD command. Furthermore, by using the /S switch, you can delete files in subdirectories derived from the specified directory. If the main directory is the starting directory, you can search an entire hard disk in this way. For example, to delete all the backup files on the hard disk with the extension .BAK, type the command and respond to the subsequent prompts as shown in Figure 7.1.

```
C:\DRDOS ---> XDEL C:\*.BAK /S

     path:  c:\
     file:  *.BAK
  WARNING:  files in subdirectories MAY BE DELETED
Is this what you wish to do (Y/N)? Y
c:\config.bak
c:\autoexec.bak
c:\savings\root.sik\mirror.bak ...delete failed
c:\freedom\bin\demo1.bak
c:\drdos\drdos.bak
c:\drdos\beispiel.bak
c:\menus\bildsch1.bak

C:\DRDOS --->
```

Figure 7.1: Deleting a group of directories with XDEL

XDEL presents the files to be deleted and prompts you to confirm (see Figure 7.1). When you enter your confirmation, XDEL starts the deleting process. If you start XDEL from a batch file, it is advisable to use the /N switch, in which case the prompt described above does not appear on the screen and XDEL immediately begins deleting.

You can use the /P switch to instruct XDEL to prompt you before deleting each individual file. The complete path name will be displayed on the screen, as in Figure 7.2, and you can decide by pressing **Y** or **N** whether each file should be deleted or not. If you use /P to allow you to confirm each deletion, XDEL will not display the common prompt for all files.

The /P switch

```
C:\DRDOS ---> XDEL C:\*.BAK /S/P
c:\config.bak (Y/N)? Y
c:\autoexec.bak (Y/N)? Y
c:\savings\root.sik\mirror.bak (Y/N)? N
c:\freedom\bin\demo1.bak (Y/N)? N
c:\drdos\drdos.bak (Y/N)? N
c:\drdos\beispiel.bak (Y/N)? Y
c:\menus\bildsch1.bak (Y/N)? Y

C:\DRDOS --->
```

Figure 7.2: Deleting a group of directories using XDEL /P

Disk Management

DR DOS employs various techniques to manage files stored on floppies and hard disks. These are partly invisible management structures such as FAT (File Allocation Table), and partly visible aids such as disk volume labels and directory and file names.

Disk Names

Each disk and hard disk can be assigned a name. This is commonly known as a *volume label*. The volume label will appear in the directory listing and can provide information about the contents and the owner of the disk. The name may be up to 11 characters long and is assigned to a disk or hard disk by the LABEL command:

LABEL

```
LABEL C:SAMPLE
```

If you don't specify the name in the command line, you will be prompted to do so:

```
LABEL C:
Volume in drive C is SCHIEB
Enter Volume label (0 to 11 characters):
```

If no name is entered, the current name will be deleted. The following symbols cannot be used in a volume label:

@ [ ] < > ( ) ^ . + = , . : * ? / \ |

To find the name of a drive, use the VOL command. VOL displays the current name on the screen. If you do not specify a drive, the name of the default drive will be displayed:

VOL

```
VOL C:
Volume in drive C is SCHIEB
```

Managing Directories

Files on floppy disks and hard disks are organized in directories to help you keep track of them. The number of directories you can have in the root directory is limited (see Table 8.1), but these in turn may contain any number of subdirectories of their own.

Drive	Maximum Number of Directories
360/720K	112
1.2/1.44Mb	224
Hard disk	512

Table 8.1: Maximum number of directories in the root directory

MD, CD,
RD

The commands MKDIR, CHDIR, and RMDIR create, change, and delete directories. MKDIR creates new directories, CHDIR changes a drive's default directory, while RMDIR removes empty directories. The commands may be abbreviated to MD, CD, and RD. Syntax is as in the following examples:

```
MD  C:\DEMO
CD  \DEMO
CD  \
RD  \DEMO
```

Alternatively, you can provide the name of the drive in question. When you invoke the CD command without parameters, you see the name of the current directory. If you type in a drive name only, the default directory of that drive will be displayed. If you want to see the default directories of all drives, type

```
CD  /A
```

Be aware that when a directory name begins with a backslash (\), it is an absolute and not a relative directory name. The directory \DRDOS is unambiguous, while DRDOS in the default directory \TEXTS would be the directory \TEXTS\DRDOS; that is, it is dependent on the current default directory.

The Tree Structure of a Disk or Hard Disk

The TREE command displays a drive's directory structure graphically. In addition, TREE can display the names of all the files stored on a disk. Syntax is as follows:

TREE

```
TREE [file] [/B] [/F] [/G] [/H] [/P]
```

File defines the directory or the files that TREE is to process. TREE's options are summarized in Table 8.2.

Option	Effect
/B	Omits file totals.
/F	Displays file names as well as directory names.
/G	Displays the directory structure in graphic format.
/H	Displays help text.
/P	TREE pauses after each full screen.

Table 8.2: The TREE command's options

In DR DOS, TREE displays the directory structure using the default directory as the starting point, unlike other DOS versions. However, it allows you to specify another directory as the starting point if you want. Use the /G switch to display the structure graphically.

Displaying the Contents of Disks or Directories

DIR displays the contents of floppies, hard disks, and directories. DIR uses a table to display the names of all files and subdirectories, their respective size in bytes, and the date and time of their last modification. Syntax is as follows:

DIR

```
DIR [file] [/A] [/C] [/D] [/L] [/N] [/P] [/R]
[/S] [/W]
```

File specifies the files to be selected. Table 8.3 summarizes DIR's options.

Option	Effect
/A	Displays all files, including system files.
/C	The specified options are set as the new default, without the command being executed.
/D	Displays only standard files, no system files.
/L	Extended display (default).
/N	No paging (default).
/P	Pauses at the end of each full screen.
/R	The command is executed and the specified options stored as the new default.
/S	Only system files are displayed.
/W	Five file names are displayed per line.

Table 8.3: The DIR command's options

Unless you specify a directory, DIR will display the contents of the current directory. You can specify certain files if you wish:

```
DIR \TEXTS\*.TXT
```

There are various options for selecting files or controlling output. A new feature of DR DOS allows you to set options as the default, so that you need not constantly repeat them. The /C option instructs DIR to store the specified options as the new default without executing the command. /R causes the command to be performed, and, at the same time, it sets the new options as the new defaults. To set the default so that the output is halted after each full screen, type

```
DIR /W /C
```

You can reverse this setting temporarily by using /N.

Extended Directory Display: XDIR

The XDIR command is an expanded version of DIR. It automatically sorts file names alphabetically before displaying them. The /T option sorts the files according to date and time, the /Z option according to size. Syntax is as below:

XDIR

```
XDIR [/H] [+|-ADHRS] [file] [/B] [/C] [/L] [/N]
[/P] [/R] [/S] [/T] [/W] [/Z]
```

File defines the files to be selected. ADHRS displays only files with (+) or without (–) a certain attribute. (If you are not familiar with attributes, see the section "Editing File Attributes" below.) Table 8.4 summarizes XDIR's options.

Option	Effect
/B	Brief display of file names and paths only.
/C	Computes and displays a hash code for each file (not for subdirectories).
/H	Displays help text.
/L	Displays all file information (default).
/P	Pauses after each screenful of display.
/R	Reverses the sorting order.
/S	Includes subdirectories.
/T	Sorts files according to date and time.
/W	Five file names are displayed per line.
/Z	Sorts files according to size.

Table 8.4: The XDIR command's options

An important feature of XDIR lets you specify attributes as selection criteria. You can also combine different attributes, which are then used as alternatives (either one or the other attribute). You can use the following attributes with XDIR:

A = Archive attribute

D = Directory attribute

H = Hidden system file attribute

R = Read-only attribute

S = System attribute

If the attribute is preceded by a plus character (+), all files with the attribute will be displayed. For example, to display only system files, type

```
XDIR +S
```

If, however, a minus character (−) precedes the attribute, the files selected in this way will not be displayed. If you want to suppress files that have an archive attribute, for example, type

```
XDIR −A
```

Alternatively, you can have XDIR compute a hash code, which can be used to detect changes made to a file. The hash code is specified in hexadecimal form (16-bit) before the file name:

```
XDIR C:\*.TXT /C
```

Two files with the same hash code are very probably identical, but not necessarily so.

Checking Floppies or Hard Disks

CHKDSK

The CHKDSK command checks floppies or hard disks for logical or physical errors. DR DOS 5.0's CHKDSK command is much more powerful than in most other DOS versions, and the command's syntax is thus more extensive:

```
CHKDSK [/H] [file] [/A] [/B] [/C] [/D] [/F]
[/L] [/M] [/P] [/R] [/S] [/V]
```

CHKDSK's options are summarized in Table 8.5.

Option	Effect
/A	Displays current memory status only.
/B	Automatically marks bad clusters.
/C	Displays the cluster number for bad files.
/D	Displays the cluster number of erased directories (in hexadecimal format).
/F	When this switch is on, the disk is modified when errors are found.
/H	Displays help text.
/L	Creates a new File Allocation Table (FAT) if necessary.
/M	Marks and displays bad clusters.
/P	Displays parent clusters for directories.
/R	Recovers the root directory and lost directories that were located in the root directory.
/S	Shows the actual space taken up by all files.
/V	Displays the names of all directories and files while CHKDSK is running.

Table 8.5: The CHKDSK command's options

If you start CHKDSK without parameters, it will check the FAT and locate clusters that are marked in the FAT as allocated, but can't be traced to any file. These "lost clusters" can be collected into files or marked as free for use.

CHKDSK reports when it locates lost clusters (see Figure 8.1). You can then specify whether you want these to be collected into files or freed as space for new files. A correction ensues only if the /F option was specified.

Lost clusters

```
D:\ ---> chkdsk C: /F
Volume BCC-HD-C1 created 20 Dec 1989 6:29

   33.454.880 bytes total disk space
      628.736 bytes in 8 hidden files
      376.832 bytes in 58 directories
   30.337.024 bytes in 1324 user files
    2.111.488 bytes available on disk

      655.360 bytes total memory
      553.696 bytes available

D:\ --->
```

Figure 8.1: A CHKDSK report

If the clusters are arranged together in chains, they will be stored as consecutively numbered files in the form FILE*nnn*.CHK, whereby one file will be created for each chain of clusters that belong together *(nnn* specifies a number starting at 000).

CHKDSK finds out how much disk space is available and how much of this is being used. The last two lines refer to the computer's conventional memory and indicate how much total memory you have available and how much of it is free.

CHKDSK lets you check to what extent the files stored on your hard disk are fragmented. If you enter specifications, only the relevant files will be checked. CHKDSK ascertains how many noncontiguous blocks a file has. If you have many files that have been allocated noncontiguous blocks, you should reorganize your disk using PC Tools or the Norton Utilities.

Renaming and Moving Files

RENAME

Every file has a file name that allows you to identify it unambiguously. Sometimes you may need to rename a file. The RENAME command (or the abbreviated version REN) lets you rename one or more files, though it cannot rename directories. The only condition for renaming a file is that the new file name doesn't already exist in the relevant directory.

For example, to change the name of the DR DOS debugger from SID to DEBUG, you would type

```
RENAME \DOS\SID.EXE DEBUG.EXE
```

The name of the directory where the file is located is specified in the source only. You can also rename a whole group of files. To rename all .BAK files as .SIK files, you would type

```
RENAME *.BAK *.SIK
```

If a file cannot be renamed, the following message will appear:

```
File already exists
```

The new file name already exists and is thus not available for use. With DR DOS 5.0, you can also use REN to move a file from one directory to another. After the move, the file will no longer exist in the source directory. In the following example, the file DEMO.DOC is renamed SAMPLE.DOC and at the same time moved to another directory:

```
REN \WORD\DEMO.DOC \WP\SAMPLE.DOC
```

Editing File Attributes

Every file has an attribute field in which certain features of the file are noted. Attributes can specify, among other things, whether a file will appear in the directory and whether it can be overwritten (see Table 8.6).

ATTRIB

Attribute	Meaning
Archive	The archive attribute shows that a file has been created or modified since the last BACKUP.
Hidden	This attribute hides the file from DIR and most programs.

Table 8.6: The file attributes

Attribute	Meaning
System	The system attribute marks system files and prevents their being edited.
Read-only	This prevents the file being deleted or overwritten.

Table 8.6: The file attributes (continued)

ATTRIB lets you change any of the four attributes allocated to a file. Depending on the character preceding it (+ or -), *R* will set or delete the read-only, *A* the archive, *H* the hidden, and *S* the system attribute. ATTRIB's syntax is as follows:

```
ATTRIB [/H] [+|-R] [+|-A] [+|-H] [+|-S] [@]file
[/P] [/S]
```

@file contains a list of *file* names. *File* defines the relevant files. Table 8.7 summarizes ATTRIB's options.

Option	Effect
/H	Displays the command's help text.
/P	Pauses after every full screen.
/S	Includes subdirectories.

Table 8.7: The ATTRIB command's options

Attributes must be defined before the file name, or ATTRIB will display the current settings of the specified attributes. If, for example, you want to remove the archive attribute from all the files on your hard disk, you can accomplish this with one command:

```
ATTRIB -A C:\*.* /S
```

The command would not affect other attributes.

You can also set and delete more than one attribute at the same time. For example, you could protect all .COM files from deletion and overwriting as follows:

```
ATTRIB -A +R C:\*.COM /S
```

Editing the Time Stamp

Every file and directory has a time and a date stamp indicating when it was last modified. The TOUCH command lets you reset these stamps. Syntax is as follows:

```
TOUCH   [/H]   [@]file   [/D:date]   [/F:E|J|U]
[/T:time] [/P] [/R] [/S]
```

TOUCH

@*file* contains a list of file names. *File* defines the relevant files. Table 8.8 summarizes TOUCH's options.

Option	Effect
/D:*date*	The new date is assigned to the specified files.
/F:*E|J|U*	Specifies European, Japanese or US date format.
/T:*time*	The new time is assigned to the specified files.
/P	Prompts before touching each file.
/R	Touches read-only files.
/S	Includes subdirectories in the touch operation.

Table 8.8: The TOUCH command's options

If you enter a file specification only, the relevant files will be allocated the current system time and date and the archive bit set as though you had just saved the files for the first time. This is advisable if you are marking files in order to create a backup copy or protect them from overwriting:

```
TOUCH C:\*.TXT /S
```

It is also possible to explicitly specify a date and time yourself in order to create a uniform directory:

```
TOUCH A:\*.* /D:7-1-1990 /T:12:00 /S
```

Recovering
Information from Corrupted Files

RECOVER

If a sector on your disk is not readable, files stored on it will not be readable either. To access at least the parts of your file that are still readable, use the RECOVER command as follows:

```
RECOVER file.nam
```

RECOVER then creates a file for each readable section of your text. These files have file names in the form FILE*nnnn*.REC, where *nnnn* specifies a number starting at 0000. If the root directory is corrupted, specify the disk only. In general, though, I would recommend that you use the Norton Utilities if you encounter corrupted files, as it provides tools much more powerful than RECOVER. It is quicker, simpler, safer, and will ultimately produce better results.

Step 9

File Output

45

The output of a file can be managed in various ways, depending on the file's contents. A plain ASCII text file can be printed using the appropriate DOS commands, whereas a database file can only be printed satisfactorily with the aid of the database itself.

Displaying the Contents of a File on the Screen

Use the TYPE command to display the contents of a file on the screen. TYPE should only be used with ASCII files, as binary files contain control characters TYPE cannot display intelligibly on the screen. Syntax is as follows:

TYPE

```
TYPE DEMO.TXT
```

If you use the wildcard characters * and ? in conjunction with TYPE, it searches for all corresponding files and displays their contents. The following example searches for all batch files:

```
TYPE *.BAT
```

When the file displays, its name appears in capital letters in the first line.

To stop the display of a lengthy file from scrolling, press Ctrl-S or Pause. Press any key to restart scrolling. Alternatively, the /P parameter—new to DR DOS 5.0—enables you to view the file one screenful at a time:

```
TYPE *.BAT /P
```

Printing ASCII Files with COPY

To print ASCII files, use the COPY command. Type **COPY**, the file name, and then type the name of the printer attached to your computer as the destination. In the following example, the destination is the default device, PRN:

```
COPY AUTOEXEC.BAT PRN
```

LPT1 or COM1 are also valid devices, depending on which port your printer is connected to (see Step 13).

You should ensure that any file you want to print does not contain any unintelligible control characters, as these can have unforeseen effects on the printer (paper wastage being one of them).

The PrtScr key

A hard copy of the current screen contents can be printed using the PrtScr key. You should be aware, though, that not every printer supports all the IBM special characters, which can distort your printout. Note that many laser printers are unsuitable for producing hard copies unless you have appropriate driver programs installed. Consult your printer handbook or other suitable literature if you encounter problems.

Switching on the Log Mode

DR DOS offers a facility for printing everything that appears on the screen. If you want the printer to log all your operations, press Ctrl-P. Everything that appears on the screen will now be sent to the printer. Ctrl-P toggles the log mode on and off. Note that the printout occurs in addition to—not in place of—the screen output.

The PRINT Command

The PRINT command is a powerful command for printing all types of files. While PRINT is printing a file, you can carry on working with other applications. For this reason, PRINT is particularly useful when you have lengthy files to print. Additionally, PRINT can hold several files in its printing queue and print these one after the other. PRINT's syntax is as follows:

```
PRINT [/H] file [/D:device]  [/B:buffer]
[/U:busy]  [/M:max]  [/S:timeslice]
[/Q:queuesize] [T/] [/C] [/P]
```

(The program line is broken to accommodate the margins of this book.) *File* specifies the files to be printed. You are allowed to use wildcards and enter more than one file name at a time. Table 9.1 gives PRINT's options.

Option	Effect
/C	The specified files are removed from the queue. If you name the file currently being printed, printing will be stopped immediately.
/H	Displays PRINT's help text.
/P	Adds the specified files to the print queue.
/T	Deletes all files from the queue and stops the current printout.
/B:*buffer*	Sets the size of the print buffer.
/D:*device*	Sends the printer output to the specified device.
/M:*max*	Sets the number of clock-ticks available for printing. The default value is 2; possibilities range from 1 to 255.
/Q:*queuesize*	Specifies the maximum number of files which can be held in the queue.
/S:*timeslice*	Describes the relative frequency with which the PRINT command is invoked. The default value is 8; values between 1 and 255 are possible.
/U:*busy*	Specifies the number of clock-ticks (a clock-tick is approximately 1/18 of a second) PRINT waits before handing back control if the printer is busy.

Table 9.1: The PRINT command's options

The parameters /B, /D, /M, /Q, /S, and /U define PRINT's working environment, that is, the size of the buffer available, how many files are to be kept there, when timeout errors should be reported, etc. Parameters are set the first time you use the PRINT utility during a DR DOS session.

If you start PRINT without specifying any parameters, certain default settings will be implemented (see Table 9.1). You must, however, specify the printing device. If you didn't include the /D parameter the first time you used PRINT, the following message will appear on the screen:

```
List device? [PRN]
PRINT:Resident portion installed
```

Press Enter to accept the default printing device PRN, or type the name of the relevant printer. You can do this the first time you issue the PRINT command by using the following syntax (in the case of LPT2):

```
PRINT /D:LPT2
```

Queue size

Other parameters let you determine what portion of your computer's time PRINT is allowed to use; however, it is usually sufficient to accept the default settings. The size of the queue is the only option you may need to alter. The /Q option allows you to specify the maximum number of files that can be accommodated in the queue. The default number of files PRINT can store in the queue is 10, which is probably sufficient for most users, but you can choose to have the queue handle between 4 and 32 files. The size of the queue must be specified the first time PRINT is used:

```
PRINT /D:LPT1 /Q:20
```

If you don't specify parameters, the current queue will be displayed on the screen. If there are no files in the queue at present, the following message will appear:

```
No files in Print queue.
```

To delete a file from the queue, type the name of the file in question after the /C parameter (for Cancel). Such options affect all the file names they precede, but not those they follow. The following example shows how you would remove the file CANCEL.TXT from the queue and print PRINT.TXT, all in one command:

```
PRINT /C CANCEL.TXT /P PRINT.TXT
```

Use the /T option to remove all files from the queue. The printing of the current file is immediately halted:

```
PRINT /T
```

Stopping all print jobs

Data security is becoming increasingly important as more users want or need to protect sensitive information from unauthorized access. It is not always easy to provide adequate data protection when a PC is operated by more than one user in an open-plan office. One of the outstanding features of DR DOS is its password-protection feature, which allows you to assign each file a set of characters you define yourself and without which the file is inaccessible—in other words, a password.

The PASSWORD Command

The PASSWORD command is used to apply password protection to files. You can assign each file a password of up to eight characters, which you need to type in to gain access to the file. There are three levels of password protection: protection from reading, from editing, and from deletion.

When you protect a file from deletion, users must type in the password in order to delete or overwrite the file, whereas anyone can read or edit it. Alternatively, you can write-protect a file, in which case it can be read without the password but not changed or deleted. Finally, in the read level, you can deny all access without the password; that is, users need it even to read the file. PASSWORD's syntax is as follows:

Levels of protection

```
PASSWORD   [H]   [@]file   [/R|/W|/P|/G[password]]
[/N] [/NP] [/NG] [/S]
```

@*file* contains a list of file names. Table 10.1 shows PASSWORD's options.

Option	Effect
/N	Removes a file's password protection.
/NG	Removes the global password.
/NP	Removes a directory's password protection.
/D:*password*	The password is required for deleting and over-writing the file.
/R:*password*	The password is required for deleting, overwriting, reading, and renaming a file, and for changing its attributes.
/W:*password*	You need the correct password to delete, over-write, or rename the file, or to change its attributes.
/G:*password*	Defines the global default password.
/P:*password*	Defines the password for a directory.

Table 10.1: The PASSWORD command's options

When you assign a password to a file, you need to use the /R, the /W, or the /D option to specify the type of protection you want. To protect a file from deletion, for example, type

```
PASSWORD DEMO.TXT /D:SECRET
```

(There is no difference between uppercase and lowercase in passwords.) The DEMO.TXT file is now protected from deletion only. You can read it, rename it, or change its attributes without the password, but you cannot delete it. If you were to try, you would get the following message:

```
DEL DEMO.TXT
File not erased: DEMO.TXT - Invalid Password
```

Accessing a Password-Protected File

To access a password-protected file, you need to type the password immediately after the file name, as in the following example:

```
DEL DEMO.TXT;SECRET
```

If you enter the wrong password, DR DOS will not allow you access to the file. To make a file completely inaccessible without the password, use the /R option:

```
PASSWORD *.TXT /R:SECRET
```

Users now need to type in the password to copy or print the file with the TYPE command:

```
TYPE DEMO.TXT;SECRET
COPY SAMPLE.TXT;SECRET A:
```

Global Passwords

It is possible to define a global password that is assigned to each password-protected file. Users will be allowed access to files only if they have the correct password. You define a global password using /G:

```
PASSWORD /G:SECRET
TYPE DEMO.TXT
```

The DEMO.TXT file is then displayed. You can remove the global default password at any time using /NG:

```
PASSWORD /NG
```

Protecting a Complete Directory

Use the /P option to password-protect an entire directory from unauthorized access:

```
PASSWORD \DEMO /P:PROTECT
```

Users now need the password to access any file in the \DEMO directory:

```
DIR \DEMO;PROTECT
TYPE \DEMO;PROTECT\ARTICLE.TXT
```

To remove a directory's password-protection, use the /NP option. PASSWORD prompts you to enter the password:

```
PASSWORD \DEMO /NP
C:\DEMO...path password? ·
```

Additional Safety Considerations

Protected files are marked in the directory where they are located, but their contents remain unchanged. This means that if the system is booted with MS-DOS or PC-DOS, the files are no longer protected. You should be aware that it is easy to gain access to protected files using auxiliary programs such as the Norton Utilities or PC Tools.

DR DOS supports several different screen modes and character tables. This step shows you how to use the available options to your best advantage.

Setting the Display Type

You can use the MODE command to select the display type. The screen modes available differ in the number of characters displayed per line and whether the screen is in monochrome or color (see Table 11.1).

MODE

Parameter	Meaning
BW40	40 characters per line, black and white display
BW80	80 characters per line, black and white display
CO40	40 characters per line, color display
CO80	80 characters per line, color display
MONO	80 characters per line, monochrome display

Table 11.1: Screen modes supported by MODE

To change screen modes, enter the code for the desired mode:

```
MODE CO80
```

You can then define the number of lines to be displayed on the screen: 25 lines for normal display, 43 for EGA, and 50 for VGA.

```
MODE CO80, 43
```

The number of columns and lines on the screen can be specified more precisely using the parameters COLS and LINES. These two parameters enable you to explicitly state the values for the console

(CON:), as in the following example:

```
MODE CON: COLS=80 LINES=50
```

Code Pages

Your computer stores five different tables defining the particular character sets required by different national languages. Without these code pages, PCs could not be used effectively in countries such as Norway. In some countries, Germany for example, there is no need to switch code pages as all the language's special characters are contained in the standard ASCII code. Table 11.2 lists the available code pages.

Code Page	Use
437	Standard IBM code (USA)
850	Multilingual
860	Portugal
862	Israel
863	French (Canada and France)
864	Middle East
865	Denmark and Norway

Table 11.2: Code pages

NLSFUNC

To work with code pages, your computer must have an EGA, VGA or MCGA adapter. Some LCD screens are also supported. You need to have the DISPLAY driver installed in the configuration file. If the above requirements are fulfilled, issue the NLSFUNC command to switch code pages:

```
NLSFUNC C:\DRDOS\COUNTRY.SYS
```

You can then select the code page to be used (see Table 11.2) using CHCP, if this was not already done in the CONFIG.SYS:

CHCP

```
CHCP 850
```

The MODE command lets you configure different code pages for each device attached to your computer (screen, printer, keyboard). If you wish to pursue this topic further, consult the *DR DOS 5.0 User Guide*, as it is too extensive to be handled here.

Displaying Characters in Graphics Mode

If you want to produce text while in graphics mode, some programs require you to copy the ASCII characters after 128 into a special buffer using the GRAFTABL command. If unintelligible symbols appear while you are working in a program's graphics mode, you should load GRAFTABL by typing

GRAFTABL

```
GRAFTABL
```

If you work with national character tables and have set the computer up for code page switching (see above), you can also use GRAFTABL to specify which code page you want to work with:

```
GRAFTABL 850
```

If you do not specify a code page, GRAFTABL and all other DR DOS commands will use the default code page 437, the US standard ASCII table.

Printing Graphics

If you are working in graphics mode and want to print a graphics display, but your application program does not offer its own hard copy routine, you should issue the GRAPHICS command. GRAPHICS installs a hard copy routine in your computer's memory capable of producing a printout even when the computer is

GRAPHICS

in graphics mode (although only on most IBM-compatible dot-matrix printers):

GRAPHICS

Use the /R option to print black and white as they appear on the screen (the default is to print what is white on your screen as black on your printer):

GRAPHICS /R

Use the COLOR option if you have a color printer attached to your system. The colors on the screen will be converted into eight different colors on the printout.

GRAPHICS COLOR

Step 12

Keyboard

The keyboard is the PC's most important input device. There are several means of assigning keyboard use. Using the ANSI device driver, you can program individual keys with character strings or commands to be performed each time you press the key.

Keyboard Layout

By default, DR DOS supports the US keyboard. The KEYB command, however, allows you to select from a range of 17 keyboards. You instruct KEYB which keyboard program should be loaded by providing a two letter code (see Table 12.1).

KEYB

Code	Country
BE	Belgium
CF	Canada (French)
DK	Denmark
FR	France
GR	Germany
IT	Italy
LA	Latin America
NL	Netherlands
NO	Norway
PO	Portugal
SF	Switzerland (French)
SG	Switzerland (German)
SP	Spain

Table 12.1: Keyboard codes supported by KEYB

Code	Country
SV	Sweden
SU	Finland
UK	United Kingdom
US	USA

Table 12.1: Keyboard codes supported by KEYB (continued)

To use the German keyboard, for example, you would type the following command:

    KEYB GR

Enhanced keyboards

KEYB recognizes automatically whether a standard or an enhanced keyboard is connected. (One of the special features of enhanced keyboards is the group of 12 function keys.) To explicitly state that you have an enhanced keyboard, use the + option after the country code:

    KEYB GR+

Similarly, use the − option to specify that you have a standard keyboard.

If you do change the default keyboard, you must also specify the code page KEYB should use (see Step 11). If you do not explicitly specify a country code, KEYB will use the country's default code page.

Assigning Values to Keys

As long as you have installed the ANSI.SYS device driver, you can assign any value you like to the keys on the keyboard. This facility is particularly useful for assigning strings to function keys and key combinations with Shift and Alt.

To reprogram a key, use the PROMPT command. PROMPT is the only command that allows you to generate the necessary control characters easily. The following is the syntax necessary to reprogram a key:

PROMPT

PROMPT $E[*keycode;newcodep*

Keycode is the code of the key whose value is to be changed. The new code is entered in quotation marks or as a decimal figure.

The code needed to reset simple keys such as *A* or *9* is the ASCII code for that character. In the case of the function keys, a two-digit code preceded by a zero is generated. At this stage, we will only deal with changing the setting of those function keys (see Table 12.2).

Key codes

FKey	Standard	Shift	Ctrl	Alt
F1	0;59	0;84	0;94	0;104
F2	0;60	0;85	0;95	0;105
F3	0;61	0;86	0;96	0;106
F4	0;62	0;87	0;97	0;107
F5	0;63	0;88	0;98	0;108
F6	0;64	0;89	0;99	0;109
F7	0;65	0;90	0;100	0;110
F8	0;66	0;91	0;101	0;111
F9	0;67	0;92	0;102	0;112
F10	0;68	0;93	0;103	0;113
F11	0;133	0;135	0;137	0;139
F12	0;134	0;136	0;138	0;140

Table 12.2: Keyboard codes for the function keys

To program the F7 key to represent the DIR command, type

```
PROMPT $e[0;65;"DIR `p
```

Each time you press F7, the DIR command will appear on the screen. To have the command executed automatically, you need only include the code for Enter (13):

```
PROMPT $e[065;"DIR "13p
```

If you want to make your key assignments permanent, you should create a suitable batch file. If you don't, the values are lost each time the computer is switched off. Also make sure that the echo mode is switched ON in the batch file. After you have entered all your definitions, the default system prompt must be redefined:

```
PROMPT $p$g
```

You can temporarily save the prompt in a batch file and redefine it as the system prompt after you have finished:

```
SET OPROMPT=%PROMPT%
PROMPT Assigning keyboard use ...
SET PROMPT=%PROMPT%
SET OPROMPT=
```

It is possible to have as many as three parallel and four serial ports available for connecting printers to your computer, which means that you can have up to seven printers connected at any given time. Normally only printers are connected to the parallel ports, while modems, a mouse, and other devices are connected to the serial ports.

Each printer, or rather, each port to which a printer is connected, is assigned a name. The first parallel port is called LPT1 or PRN, the second, LPT2, and the third, LPT3. The first serial port is COM1 or AUX, the last, COM4.

Device names

Setting Up Serial Printers

If you want to connect a serial printer, you must prepare DR DOS to use it. First, you must program the relevant communications parameters for the port. The command you use is

```
MODE COMn:
 baudrate[,[parity],[databits],[stopbits][,P]]
```

The first parameter defines the baud rate, that is, the rate at which information is communicated in bits per second. The following baud rates are possible: 110, 150, 300, 600, 1200, 2400, 4800, 9600 and 19200. Following the baud rate, the parity is defined: it can be N, O, or E (none, odd, or even). After that, you specify the number of databits (7 or 8) and stopbits (1 or 2). If you include the P option at the end, timeout errors will be ignored.

Baud rate

Redirecting Output to a Serial Port

You can also use the MODE command to reassign LPT ports to serial ports. This redirects the output of programs that use one of the LPT ports to a serial port, thus allowing programs that don't support serial ports to access serial printers. You just have to state the name of the parallel and the serial ports as follows:

```
MODE LPTn:=COMn:
```

If you were to reassign LPT1 to COM1, for example, output would be redirected from the parallel port LPT1 to the serial port COM1, enabling you to access the printer connected to the COM1 port. To return to the default settings, you would enter

```
MODE LPT1
```

Step 14

RAM Disk

A RAM disk is a virtual drive (as opposed to a physical drive). It can be set up alongside floppy disk and hard disk drives. The chief advantage of a RAM disk is its very fast access time: it is approximately 100 times faster than the fastest hard disk. On the other hand, however, RAM disks don't have a permanent memory. Everything stored "on" them is lost when the computer is switched off. RAM disks are therefore suitable for temporary storage and as read-only drives.

Virtual drives

RAM disk drives can be set up only in the CONFIG.SYS file—and not during a working session. You can set up as many RAM disks as you have memory available for. If your system has less than 640K RAM, it is not advisable to use a RAM disk. You should only use a RAM disk if you have more than 640K and make use of the extended (but not expanded) memory above the 1Mb barrier.

To create a RAM disk, you use the VDISK device driver, which can be installed with the DR DOS SETUP program. Type

```
DEVICE=VDISK.SYS [disk size [sector size
[maximum number of files [/E:sectors]]]]
```

Disk size defines the size of the RAM disk in kilobytes. If you don't have extended memory, the RAM disk is restricted to 256K. *Sector size* specifies the size of the RAM disk sectors as 128, 256, or 512 bytes. *Maximum number of files* specifies how many files are to be accommodated in the root directory of the RAM disk. This number can be between 2 and 512; the default value is 64. The /E:*sectors* option locates the RAM disk in the computer's extended memory (above the 1 Mb barrier). The sectors option defines how many sectors are read at once. The possibilities range from 1 to 8, 8 being the default setting.

A RAM disk is assigned the next free drive identifier letter. Data relevant to the RAM disk, including the drive letter, is displayed when the computer is booted.

RAM disks are most useful for storing files you need to access frequently, such as batch files. You must remember, though, to include the RAM disk in your search path (see the PATH command). When you copy the command processor (COMMAND.COM) to a RAM disk, define the appropriate name for the environment variable COMSPEC:

```
COPY C:\DRDOS\COMMAND.COM E:SET
COMSPEC=E:COMMAND.COM
```

Step 15

EDITOR

 15

DR DOS includes a convenient full-screen editor that allows you to create and edit ASCII texts. In some ways, EDITOR, as it is known, resembles older WordStar versions, and users familiar with WordStar will notice the similarity. With version 5.0, you can highlight, copy, move, delete and save blocks of text, just as you can in WordStar. You can also enter ASCII characters with values higher than 127, which was not possible before.

EDITOR permits you to edit ASCII files only; it cannot handle binary files. You can specify the name of the file you want to edit when you start EDITOR:

```
EDITOR \AUTOEXEC.BAT
```

If the file doesn't exist, EDITOR asks whether it should create it:

```
C:\AUTOEXEC.BAT ...file not found
Create new file (Y/N)?
```

The same message appears on the screen if you try to load a file that doesn't exist while working with EDITOR. If you press **Y,** EDITOR will create a new file for immediate use.

EDITOR provides several help screens that can be displayed by pressing F1 or Ctrl-J. You can choose to keep a quick reference display on the screen after reading all of the help pages. However, the summary, which appears in the upper part of the screen, reduces the area free for editing.

Help screen

Table 15.1 shows the functions of EDITOR's key combinations.

Key(s)	Function
↑	Cursor moves up a line.
↓	Cursor moves down a line.

Table 15.1: EDITOR's key combinations

Key(s)	Function
→	Cursor moves one character to the right.
←	Cursor moves one character to the left.
PgUp	Moves to previous page.
PgDn	Moves to next page.
Del	Deletes the character under the cursor.
Backspace	Deletes the character to the left of the cursor.
Ctrl-A	Moves the cursor back one word.
Ctrl-F	Moves the cursor forward one word.
Ctrl-J	Displays help text.
Ctrl-T	Deletes from the cursor to the end of the word.
Ctrl-Y	Deletes the line the cursor is in.
Ctrl-KB	Starts a block highlight.
Ctrl-KK	Ends a block highlight.
Ctrl-KC	Copies a block to the cursor position.
Ctrl-KL	Loads a text block.
Ctrl-KM	Moves block to the cursor position.
Ctrl-KW	Saves a block.
Ctrl-KY	Deletes a block.
Ctrl-KD	Saves a file and prompts for a new file name to edit.
Ctrl-KQ	File not saved, leaves EDITOR.
Ctrl-KS	Saves file.
Ctrl-KX	Saves file and leaves EDITOR.
Ctrl-QC	Moves cursor to end of file.
Ctrl-QR	Moves cursor to start of file.

Table 15.1: EDITOR's key combinations (continued)

Pipes and Filters

15

The majority of DOS commands display their results on the screen (the standard output device) and receive information from the keyboard (the standard input device). The default input and output devices can be changed by redirection commands. You can, for example, print a directory listing you display with DIR.

Commands for Redirecting

Use the redirection symbol (>) to redirect the output of a DOS command or an application program. You can redirect your information to a file or to a device attached to your computer. To print a directory listing on the printer (in this case PRN), type in

```
DIR >PRN
```

The redirection command must be the last command in the command line, but it doesn't impose restrictions on the preceding DOS commands. You can use all the options and parameters you normally use. The output of all DOS commands can be redirected in this way.

If you redirect output to a file instead of displaying it on the screen, an appropriate file will be created automatically. If a file with the same name already exists, it will be overwritten unless you use the redirection symbol, >>. Thus, if you issue the command

```
DIR *.DOC >LIST.LST
```

and then issue the command

```
DIR *.BAK >>LIST.LST
```

the names of all .DOC and .BAK files in the current directory will appear in the LIST.LST file.

You can also use redirection commands to redirect the contents of a file as input for a command. This facility can be very useful in situations where the user would normally be bothered unnecessarily with system prompts. All the required input must be listed in such a file, for the computer will crash as soon as one single prompt is not answered properly as the keyboard is blocked. For example, to assign the name stored in the file NAME.DOC to the hard disk, you would proceed as follows:

```
LABEL C: <NAME.DOC
```

The contents of the NAME.DOC file could be

```
HARDDISK
```

Remember to press Enter before you end the file.

Combining DOS Commands

The piping symbol

You can combine different DOS commands using the piping symbol. However, not all commands are suitable for piping, only the few filter commands. To combine two DOS commands, use the piping symbol, as shown below

```
DIR|SORT|MORE
```

DOS stores the output of the first command in a temporary file, which is subsequently handed over to the second command. The second command reads its input from the temporary file and so on. Now let's take a look at the three best known filter commands.

MORE

Displaying output a screen at a time

The MORE command displays output one screenful at a time. A message indicating that you can press any key to display the next screenful appears at the bottom of each screen. To display a long directory, one screenful at a time, you would type

```
DIR|MORE
```

You will probably not use MORE all that frequently, as most DOS commands have an option available that will display output a screenful at a time. However, where this is not possible, you can use MORE.

FIND

FIND searches in a file for a string of characters you specify, and once these characters are found, it displays the lines containing the search string. You can use switches to have the displayed lines numbered, to differentiate between uppercase and lowercase, to include subdirectories in the search process, or to display only the lines that do not include the search string. Syntax is as follows:

```
FIND [/H] [/C] [/N] [/S] [/U] [/V] "search
string" [file]
```

"Search string" defines the string to be searched for. Uppercase and lowercase distinctions are not taken into consideration. *File* can be used to define the name of the file in which the string is to be sought if you are not using FIND as a filter. The file names can contain wildcards. Table 16.1 summarizes FIND's options.

Option	Effect
/C	Shows only the relevant lincs.
/H	Displays help text.
/N	Displays line numbers.
/S	Searches files in subdirectories.
/U	Takes case into account while searching.
/V	Displays the lines not containing the string.

Table 16.1: The FIND command's options

If FIND is used as a filter, it reads from the output of the previous DOS command. For example, if you want to display files edited on 6/3/1990, use FIND as follows:

```
DIR¦FIND "6/03/90"
```

Note that FIND can also be used as a normal DOS command. In this case, the relevant file name needs to be specified as the last item in the command line (see syntax).

SORT

SORT sorts the contents of an ASCII file line by line according to ASCII code, and then it writes the file to the standard output device. Syntax is as follows:

```
SORT [/H] [/R] [/+column]
```

SORT's options are summarized in Table 16.2.

Option	Effect
/H	Displays help text.
/R	Reverses the order of sorting (*b* before *a*).
/+	Specifies the column a sort should start on.

Table 16.2: The SORT command's options

Specifying a starting point for SORT

SORT generally works through the file one line at a time and takes all characters in the line into account. Using the /+ option, however, you can make the sort start on a certain column. This enables you to sort according to different criteria, assuming you have fixed line formats. For example, to sort a normal directory alphabetically, type

```
DIR¦SORT
```

If, however, you want the files to be arranged according to size, have SORT start at column 13:

```
DIR¦SORT /+13
```

If SORT is not being used as a filter, you must use redirection symbols. Input and output files must never be identical:

```
SORT <CLIENT.LST >CLIENT.SOR
```

Hard disks are high-capacity storage media, and as such, they require skillful management by the operating system. A hard disk can be separated into as many as four independent sections, known as *partitions*. Each partition can be assigned a different operating system: for example, XENIX in one, DOS in another, and so on. Only one partition can be active at a time; that is, you can boot from the active partition only. Normally, however, only one operating system is installed on a hard disk anyway, so you only need to create one partition. DR DOS can handle primary partitions up to 512Mb in size, setting it apart from MS/PC-DOS versions up to and including DOS 3.3, which only support primary partitions up to 32Mb.

Partitions

FDISK is the utility used to partition and format a hard disk. In DR DOS, you can format a hard disk only with FDISK (unless you buy special auxiliary programs). However, preformatting, which is the first step you must take when installing a hard disk, can't be performed by FDISK; you need a program such as Disk Manager or SpeedStor to do this.

FDISK

Creating a Partition

FDISK is a menu-driven utility; that is, a menu from which you can select items is displayed on the screen (see Figure 17.1). Select the first option to create a partition. A word of warning though: if you have more than one hard disk installed on your system, you need to use the fourth menu option to select the appropriate drive.

Primary Partitions

When creating partitions, you must distinguish between primary and extended partitions. You must create at least one primary partition to work with DR DOS, as the system can only be booted from a primary partition. If you attempt to create a primary partition when one already exists, an error message will be displayed.

```
FDISK R1.43    Fixed Disk Maintenance Utility
Copyright (c) 1986,1988,1990 Digital Research Inc. All rights reserved.

Partitions on 1st hard disk (85.0 Mb, 85 cylinders):
No  Drive  Start  End   MB    Status  Type
 1   C:      0     31   31.9    A     DOS 3.0
 2   --     32     84   53.0    N     DOS EXT




Select options:
1) Create DOS partition
2) Delete DOS partition
3) Select bootable partition
4) Display logical drives in extended partition

Enter desired option: (ESC = exit) [?]
```

Figure 17.1: The FDISK menu

Changing the size of a partition

To change the size of an existing partition, you must first delete it. If you are creating a partition for the first time, you can specify its size. DR DOS assumes you want to reserve the entire available space on the hard disk for the partition. If this is the case, simply press **Y** when you see this prompt:

Use cylinders 0-613 for DOS (20.3 Mbytes) (Y/N)?

If, however, you do not want to use all the available space for a partition, you must specify the cylinders where the partition should start and end. You can't specify the size as a percentage or in megabytes; you must calculate how many cylinders are needed:

Enter starting cylinder:0
Enter ending cylinder (9-613):

Assigning a name to a partition

FDISK then establishes the number of available memory blocks and checks each one for defects. The partition is formatted during the check. Once the formatting is complete, you are prompted to assign the new partition a name, which can be up to 11 characters long:

```
Enter disk label:
```

Extended Partitions

You need to create an extended DOS partition in DR DOS only if you want to divide the hard disk space into separate logical drives. If this is the case, you can create an extended DOS partition alongside the primary one. The operating system itself must always be located in the primary DOS partition, as it can only be booted from there. Basically, the same rules that apply to a primary DOS partition apply to creating an extended DOS partition, except that the extended DOS partition has to be separated into different logical drives afterwards.

You can divide an extended DOS partition into as many logical drives as you want. You define the size of the logical drives in cylinders. The identifying letters of the new logical drives appear on the screen as they are defined. You give a logical drive a volume label once you have created the drive.

Logical Drives

Deleting a DOS Partition

To delete a DOS partition, select the second menu option from the screen shown in Figure 17.1. You must specify whether you want to delete a primary partition, an extended partition, or a logical drive. Be aware that when you delete a drive, all the information stored on it is also deleted. You should make backup copies of your files beforehand if you don't want to lose them.

Once you have selected the Delete DOS Partition option, all the logical drives or partitions you have created are numbered and displayed on the screen. You are prompted to type in the number of the partition you want to delete (see Figure 17.2). DR DOS prompts you once again to ensure that no partition is removed by mistake.

```
FDISK R1.43    Fixed Disk Maintenance Utility
Copyright (c) 1986,1988,1990 Digital Research Inc. All rights reserved.

Partitions on 1st hard disk (85.0 Mb, 85 cylinders):
No  Drive  Start  End    MB    Status  Type
1   C:     0      31     31.9  A       DOS 3.0
2   --     32     84     53.0  N       DOS EXT




Enter number of partition to delete: (ESC = exit) [? ]
```

Figure 17.2: Deleting a partition

Activating a Partition

When your computer is booted, the primary partition in your hard disk is activated and the operating system in that partition is started. Only one partition can be active at a time. If you only use DR DOS, the primary DOS partition will, of course, always be active. Only the primary DOS partition can be used to boot the system.

Leaving FDISK

Once you have made all your changes, you can leave FDISK. If you have altered the partitions, you will be prompted to reload DR DOS:

```
Insert a DR DOS system diskette into your
diskette drive and switch the computer on.
The operating system must now be copied.
```

Step 18

SID Debugging Tool

The SID debugger (Symbolic Information Debugger) enables you to process binary files. You can use it, for example, to patch program files. However, SID must be used with great care, as it can make programs inoperative. It is also possible to destroy data on a disk with SID.

You specify which file you want to debug when you start SID. The following example illustrates SID's syntax; however, you should not enter it as it could cause undesirable effects (the address of the format code varies from one XT hard controller to another).

```
SID CHKDSK.COM
```

SID can be used to preformat the hard disk installed on XTs. To do this, just start the relevant formatting routine. Unlike MS/PC-DOS's DEBUG, the program is started without an equals sign:

Preformatting with SID

```
GC800:5
```

Consult your hard disk manual to find out the start address for the preformatting routine if necessary.

Table 18.1 describes SID commands and their valid parameters. (Some command lines in this table are broken to accommodate the margins of this book; when entering these commands, you would type them on one line.)

Command	Effect
?	Lists SID commands.
??	Displays SID command conventions.
=	Displays currently defined macros.

Table 18.1: SID commands and their parameters

Command	Effect
:name	Definition of a macro.
=name	Executes the macro *name*.
A[*address*]	Assembles from the specified or current address.
B*address1,endaddress1, address2*	Compares *endaddress1* bytes of memory starting at *address1* with that starting at *address2* and displays discrepancies.
D[W]*startaddress* [*endaddress*]	Displays a memory dump from *startaddress* to *endaddress* in the form of hexadecimal values, whereby you can choose between byte or word values if DW is specified. If you don't specify an end address, 12 lines of data will be displayed.
E[*file*][[-]*symbolfile*...]	Loads the specified file as well as the relevant symbol file. If you don't specify a file name, all memory being used by SID for programs is released.
F[W]*address,endaddress, value*	Fills a memory area from *address* to *endaddress* with a value. If FW is specified, a word value will be used, otherwise it will be a byte value.
[-]G *startaddress* [,*b1*,[,*b2*[,...]]]	Starts a program at the startaddress and defines breakpoints at up to ten addresses. When the command is

Table 18.1: SID commands and their parameters (continued)

Command	Effect
	preceded by a hyphen, messages will be suppressed.
H[*value1*[,*value2*]]	Displays the value of a symbol or calculates the sum, difference, product and quotient of the two values. When it is used with one parameter, it returns the hexadecimal value as well as the ASCII character.
I*parameter*	Defines the parameter line for a machine program.
[-]L[*address*[,*length*]]	Disassembles the memory area starting from *address*. Thirty-two bytes will be disassembled unless you specify length. When the command is preceded by a hyphen, no symbol values are displayed.
M*address1*,*length*, *address2*	Copies the memory area between *address1* and *address2*, taking length and direction into consideration.
[-]P[*address*[,*value*]]	Displays, sets, and clears all passpoints (passpoints are break points that you do not have to set each time you enter the G command). By defining a value, you may select how often the instruction at the breakpoint executes before control is handed back to the console.

Table 18.1: SID commands and their parameters (continued)

Command	Effect
Q[I|O][W][*port*[,*value*]]	The command reads (I) data from a port or writes (O) data to a port. The date may be in byte or word form (W).
Q[R|W] *address,drive, sector,number*	QR and QW enable you to read and write data from sectors. The start address of the memory area, the drive, the sector number and the number of sectors into which or from which data is to be written are defined.
R *filename*[,*address*]	Loads the file into a block of memory starting from an optional address.
[-]S	Displays or suppresses (-) the segment registers.
SR *address,endaddress, search values*	Searches the memory block starting at *address* for a list of values (or character strings).
S[W]*address*	Edits the contents of memory locations, word by word if you specify SW.
[-]T[W][*number*]	Trace mode. If a hyphen precedes the command, symbol values will be suppressed. If W is specified, subprograms are also traced. You can define how many program steps should be executed with *number.*

Table 18.1: SID commands and their parameters (continued)

Command	Effect
[-]U[W][*number*]	This command works like T, the only difference being that the contents of the CPU state are displayed before the first step only.
V	Displays program data (start and end addresses).
W *filename*[,*address* [,*endaddress*]]	Writes the contents of the defined block of memory to disk as a file with the name *filename*.
X[*register*][*flag*]	Displays the contents of CPU registers or flags.
Z	Displays the registers of the attached math coprocessor.

Table 18.1: SID commands and their parameters (continued)

Batch files normally consist of a sequence of DOS commands executed in turn. To execute all the commands, all you have to do is start the appropriate batch file. All DOS commands can be used in batch files, and applications can be started from them.

Creating Batch Files

To create a batch file, use a word processor of your choice or EDITOR. Note, however, that batch files are stored in ASCII format; they must be in plain text, without formatting control characters. The file extension for batch files is .BAT.

You start a batch file by entering its file name. It is loaded and started like any other command file. You can stop a batch file at any time while it is running by pressing Ctrl-C. A message appears on the screen asking whether you really want to halt the batch file. If you reply in the negative, the file will continue to be executed; pressing **Y** will cause it to be halted.

Starting and stopping batch files

The AUTOEXEC.BAT file, which is automatically started when the computer is booted, must be stored either in the root directory of the first hard disk drive or in the floppy drive the system is started from for DR DOS to find it. The commands stored in AUTOEXEC.BAT are executed one after the other each time the system is started.

AUTO-EXEC.BAT

Batch File Subcommands

You can use special subcommands in batch files to help run them. Invoking these subcommands causes batch files to resemble simple programs that can make decisions.

When a batch file is started, the ECHO mode, which causes each command in the file to be displayed on the screen, is active. To disable ECHO mode, use the ECHO command. ECHO mode can be reactivated at any time.

It is also possible to explicitly inhibit the display of individual commands, irrespective of the current status of ECHO mode. This is done by placing the @ character before the relevant command:

```
@ECHO OFF
```

Displaying Messages with ECHO

ECHO displays messages on the screen. If no text is specified, ECHO displays the current status of ECHO mode. ECHO mode is set with ON and OFF:

```
ECHO OFF
ECHO This is a message.
ECHO This will be printed! >PRN
```

Sending text to a printer

As the last example shows, ECHO can be used to send a text to the printer (see Step 16). (You can also specify a file to which the text should be written.)

Creating Loops with FOR

FOR allows repetitive execution of a command for each value in a list. FOR's syntax is as follows:

```
FOR %%variable IN (list) DO command %%a
```

DO ensures that the ensuing command is executed as often as there are values in the list. You can only have one command after DO.

If more than one command is to be executed, you should load and run a second batch file with CALL. It is important that the loop results are actually used:

```
FOR %%A IN (*.*) DO TREE %%A >PRN
```

If wildcards are used in the list, DOS substitutes variables sequentially with each individual filename found:

```
FOR %%A IN (*.*) DO ECHO %%A Gotcha!
```

Jumping with GOTO

GOTO allows you to move to a specific label in the batch file and thus control the running of a program:

```
GOTO NoDisk
```

GOTO is generally used in conjunction with IF to execute a conditional program branch. Labels appear singly in a command line and are introduced by a colon.

Conditional Execution of Commands with IF

Conditional processing means that a command will only be executed under certain conditions. IF can check if a file exists, compare two character strings, and check the ERRORLEVEL system variable. The syntax of IF is

```
IF [NOT] condition command
```

NOT reverses a condition; that is, the following command is executed only if the condition is false. *Command* is a normal DOS command, often the GOTO command. *Condition* is one of the following three possibilities:

NOT

string1==string2	The condition is true if the two character strings are identical.
EXIST *filename*	The condition is true if the specified file exists.
ERRORLEVEL *number*	If the system variable ERRORLEVEL is a greater than or equals number, the condition is true.

The following example illustrates how conditional processing is used. If the file LIST.LST doesn't exist, it obviously can't be deleted, in which case the corresponding command is overlooked (and an error message thus prevented).

```
@ECHO OFF
IF NOT EXIST LIST.LST GOTO Next
DEL LIST.LST
:Next
ECHO N|CHKDSK /V
```

ERROR-LEVEL

Most programs have an exit code, which is assigned to the system variable ERRORLEVEL. The exit code indicates whether a program was closed successfully or with errors:

```
@ECHO OFF
BACKUP *.COM A:
IF NOT ERRORLEVEL 1 GOTO OK
ECHO BACKUP
ended with an error
:OK
```

Subprograms and Parameters

You can place parameters into a batch file when you activate the file in the command line. The parameters are stored as replacement variables %1 through %9. If you want to define more than nine parameters, the list has to be shifted to accommodate the extra parameters. A parameter that doesn't exist can be ascertained easily using IF, as shown in the second line of the following example. The SHIFT command moves the parameters on the command line one position to the left, whereby the first parameter is lost.

```
@ECHO OFF
IF /%1==/ GOTO End
:Next
ECHO Parameter found: %1
SHIFT
```

```
GOTO Next
:End
```

It is possible to start a second batch file from the original one. However, it is not sufficient to simply state the name of the second batch file; you need to use the CALL command. In other words, control is not handed back to the original batch file. To start a second batch file as a subprogram, use the CALL command:

Starting a subprogram

```
FOR %%A IN (A B C D E) DO CALL WORKWITH %%A
```

As you see, you can also issue parameters to the batch file using CALL. Again, these are available from %1 through %9.

You can call up as many batch files from the original one as you like, so long as you have enough memory.

Your batch file can also include current variables in the DR DOS environment. These must be enclosed in percentage signs:

```
ECHO The search path is %PATH%
ECHO You are using %OS% %VER%
```

Loading Resident Programs

If you want to load a resident program into the AUTOEXEC file and upper memory is theoretically available (see Step 20), you can load the TSR commands CURSOR.EXE, KEYB.COM, NLSFUNC.EXE, GRAPHICS.COM, GRAFTABLE.COM, JOIN.EXE, and SHARE.EXE into upper memory using HI-LOAD:

```
HILOAD KEYB GR-
```

You may also be able to load some third-party TSRs into upper memory.

Step 20

The Configuration File

The configuration you want for your system is specified in the configuration file CONFIG.SYS. With its SETUP command, DR DOS provides you with a handy tool for modifying the CONFIG.SYS file. However, experienced users generally prefer to modify CONFIG.SYS manually by placing special commands within the file. This step describes these commands and their uses.

?

When a command line begins with a question mark, you are asked during booting whether or not the command line should be executed. You can use the question mark to define text you want to have displayed (note, however, that a command line may not exceed 128 characters):

Conditional execution

```
? FILES=20
? "Install ANSI?" DEVICE=\DOS\ANSI.SYS
```

BREAK

The BREAK option determines whether you can stop a running program by pressing Ctrl-Break. Programs and commands can be stopped during disk access only if you set BREAK to ON.

Ctrl-Break

BUFFERS

BUFFERS defines how many buffers are available for data transfer between DOS and the floppy disk and hard disk drives. Five hundred twelve bytes are reserved per buffer and you can install up to 99 buffers. Normally, it is advisable to use between 15 and 30.

CHAIN

The CHAIN command transfers control to another configuration file. This allows you to execute predefined CONFIG files or, alternatively, start them by using a question mark. The current configuration file is closed and not further interpreted after the new CONFIG file is executed.

```
FILES=20
?"Alternative CONFIG?" CHAIN=\DOS\CONEW.SYS
```

COUNTRY

Country
code

The COUNTRY command defines the country code. This code is instrumental in setting the date format and other values appropriate for your country. You can also select the code page you want to use as a default, unless the default value is already set for your country. The third parameter you must specify is the file name of the auxiliary file where COUNTRY can find the information it needs. This is generally the COUNTRY.SYS file in the system directory.

A typical COUNTRY command line in German-speaking countries, for example, would look like this:

```
COUNTRY=049,,C:\DRDOS\COUNTRY.SYS
```

Table 20.1 lists the country codes.

Country	*Code*
Australia	061
Belgium	032
Canada(French)	002

Table 20.1: Country codes

Country	Code
Denmark	045
Finland	358
France	033
Germany	049
Israel	972
Italy	039
Japan	081
Latin America	003
Middle East	785
Netherlands	031
Portugal	351
Spain	034
Sweden	046
Switzerland (German)	041
Switzerland (French)	041
United Kingdom	044
USA	001

Table 20.1: Country codes (continued)

DEVICE

The DEVICE command allows you to install device drivers. Device drivers usually have the extension .SYS and are used to operate your mouse or other peripherals. DEVICE can be used to install the standard device drivers shown in Table 20.2.

Device drivers

Driver	Function
ANSI.SYS	Provides extra options for your screen.
CACHE.EXE	Optimizes disk access.
DISPLAY.SYS	Screen driver for code pages.
DRIVER.SYS	Device driver for external disk drives.
EMM386.SYS	EMS driver for 386-based computers.
EMMXMA.SYS	Expanded memory driver for ATs.
HIDOS.SYS	Manages expanded memory on ATs.
PRINTER.SYS	Printer driver for code pages.
VDISK.SYS	Device driver for RAM disks.

Table 20.2: Optional device drivers supported by DR DOS

DRIVPARM

This command enables you to reset the specifications for a physical disk drive. DRIVPARM is used similarly to DRIVER.SYS, the difference being that DRIVPARM allows you to modify drives already known to DR DOS, while DRIVER.SYS defines new drives. Syntax is as follows:

```
DRIVPARM=/D:d [/C] [/F:f] [/H:h] [/N] [/S:s]
[/T:t]
```

Table 20.3 summarizes DRIVEPARM's options.

Option	Effect
/D:d	Defines the drive's letter with 0=A,1=B.
/C	Drive is able to detect a change of disk in the drive.

Table 20.3: The DRIVPARM command's options

Option	Effect
/F:*f*	Specifies the drive type as 0=360 K, 1=1.2 Mb, 2=720K and 7=1.44Mb.
/H:*h*	Specifies the number of drive heads.
/N	The drive cannot be changed.
/S:*s*	Defines the number of sectors per track.
/T:*t*	Defines the number of tracks.

Table 20.3: The DRIVPARM command's options (continued)

ECHO

ECHO can be used to display of messages on the screen during startup. ECHO is particularly useful when used in conjunction with ?:

```
ECHO Are 25 DOS buffers sufficient?
?"Files = 25" Files=25
```

FASTOPEN

FASTOPEN reduces the time needed to access files on the installed hard disks by temporarily storing details of all the previous times files were accessed. If a file is accessed repeatedly, access to it becomes faster. FASTOPEN can store between 128 and 32,768 file names. The default is 512:

```
FASTOPEN=512
```

FCBS

FCBS specifies the number of files that can be opened at the same time. MS/PC-DOS versions from 2.11 on use file handlers as well as FCBS to manage files, and most programs on the market today favor file handlers. The first parameter of FCBS defines the maximum number of files that can be opened simultaneously (up to 255) and the second specifies how many of these are protected from automatic closure (up to 255). The following values are usually adequate:

```
FCBS=10,10
```

FILES

The FILES command specifies how many files can be opened at once. The default in DR DOS is 20, but it is possible to select a number up to 255. It is generally advisable to set the value between 20 and 30 (48 bytes per open file):

```
FILES=25
```

HIDEVICE

Special device drivers

Like DEVICE, HIDEVICE serves to install device drivers, but HIDEVICE tries to load the device driver specified into upper memory. Before using HIDEVICE, you must have a device driver loaded that supports upper memory, such as EMM386.SYS. HIDEVICE can load the ANSI.SYS, CACHE.EXE and VDISK.SYS drivers into upper memory. Syntax is as follows:

```
HIDEVICE=C:\DOS\ANSI.SYS
```

HIDOS

HIDOS is used to relocate as much of DR DOS as possible into upper memory. This is only possible if an appropriate device driver—for example, EMM386.SYS or HIDOS.SYS—is loaded first. The default for HIDOS is OFF. Activate the option with the full command:

```
HIDOS=ON
```

HIINSTALL

Like INSTALL, HIINSTALL loads a program during startup, but also tries to load it in upper memory, thereby saving space in conventional memory. Before using HIINSTALL, you must have a device driver which supports upper memory loaded, such as EMM386.SYS. The following DR DOS programs can be loaded into upper memory:

CURSOR.EXE	GRAFTABL.COM
KEYB.COM	PRINT.EXE
NLSFUNC.EXE	SHARE.EXE
GRAPHICS.COM	

In order, for example, to load the keyboard driver into upper memory, use the following command:

```
HIINSTALL=C:\DOS\KEYB.COM GR
```

HISTORY

HISTORY enables you to extend DR DOS's editing facilities (see Step 3). Each command you enter is temporarily stored in a special memory buffer where it can be edited. HISTORY creates two buffers, the size of which you specify with the second parameter. The last parameter sets the insert mode ON or OFF. If the first parameter is OFF, HISTORY is not active. Syntax is as follows:

Convenient editing

```
HISTORY=ON,512,ON
```

INSTALL

INSTALL allows you to load a program into the CONFIG file and store it in conventional memory. The following DOS commands can be installed with INSTALL:

CURSOR.EXE	GRAFTABL.COM
KEYB.COM	PRINT.EXE
NLSFUNC.EXE	SHARE.EXE
GRAPHICS.COM	

You can, of course, include options:

```
INSTALL=C:\DOS\KEYB.GR
```

LASTDRIVE

With LASTDRIVE, you define the last drive letter possible. DR DOS detects during the startup procedure how many physical and logical drives are required. If, however, you want to explicitly define the last drive, you can do so using LASTDRIVE:

```
LASTDRIVE=J
```

REM

Remarks

The REM command allows you to include remarks in the CONFIG file that do not affect the file's execution:

```
REM Loading the ANSI.SYS device driver
```

SHELL

The command processor

SHELL loads the command processor. This is also done automatically, but SHELL provides you with the option of specifying the size of the environment or loading an alternative command processor:

```
SHELL=C:\DOS\COMMAND.COM /P /E:512
```

By using the /P switch, you can choose to have COMMAND.COM permanently installed in memory. /E specifies the size of the environment: 512 bytes is normally adequate.

The Device Drivers

You can install different device drivers using DEVICE and HIDE-VICE. The following sections provide brief descriptions of the device drivers available in DR DOS.

ANSI.SYS

ANSI.SYS is an extended device driver for screen and keyboard. You can reprogram your keyboard or access special escape sequences only if you have this driver loaded. (See Step 12 for more details on ANSI.SYS.)

CACHE.EXE

CACHE.EXE optimizes disk access by keeping commonly read in memory. The larger the available buffer, the more data it can store, thus causing the disks to be accessed less often. This naturally enhances your computer's speed. CACHE can be installed as a device driver or set up at the DR DOS command line. Syntax is as follows:

```
CACHE [/H] [/S=xxx] [/E] [/X]
```

Table 20.4 summarizes CACHE's options.

Option	Effect
/H	Displays help text.
/S:xxx	Specifies buffer size in kilobytes.
/E	Uses extended memory for buffers.
/X	Uses expanded memory for buffers.

Table 20.4: The CACHE command's options

To specify a cache of 200K in extended memory, you would use the following command:

```
DEVICE=C:\DRDOS\CACHE.EXE /E /S:200
```

DISPLAY.SYS

You need to use DISPLAY as a screen driver if you want to use code pages. The following command is generally required:

```
DEVICE=C:\DRDOS\DISPLAY.SYS CON=(,,2)
```

DRIVER.SYS

DRIVER.SYS enables you to create an additional logical drive. The parameters for the logical drive correspond exactly to those described under DRIVPARM.

EMM386.SYS

Expanded memory

You can turn extended memory on computers with 80386 or 80486 processors into expanded memory using EMM386.SYS. This driver should be installed in the CONFIG file before any other drivers that use extended memory. To use EMM386.SYS, load SETUP and activate the appropriate option. Everything else happens automatically. The options possible with this driver are discussed in Appendix A.

EMMXMA.SYS

EMMXMA.SYS is used to facilitate the use of memory expansion cards configured as expanded memory in DR DOS. This is only possible with PS/2 models 50, 50Z, and 60. The syntax for EMMXMA.SYS is as follows:

```
DEVICE=EMMXMA.SYS [/FRAMExxxx] [/KB=ddd]
```

EMS size

The /FRAME option specifies the start address of the 64K mapping window. If this option is missing, EMMXMA automatically searches for a free window. /KB allows you to define how much memory should be allocated as EMS 4.0. If this option is not specified, all available memory will be used.

HIDOS.SYS

HIDOS.SYS allows the extended memory of 80286-based computers to be used in DR DOS. Parts of DR DOS may be relocated to upper memory. The device driver also allows users with computers based on Neat Chip sets to use the upper memory between 640K and 1Mb for drivers and TSR programs, which leaves more space free in the conventional memory.

Use the HIINSTALL, HIDEVICE, and HILOAD commands to relocate device drives into upper memory. HIDOS automatically recognizes if such memory areas are available. If you want to use HIDOS, load SETUP and activate the relevant options. The rest is done automatically.

PRINTER.SYS

If you have an IBM model 4201, 4208, or 5205 and you want to use code pages, you have to use PRINTER.SYS to drive your printer. You should be aware that only these printers support the use of code pages. The following command is the one generally used:

```
DEVICE=C:\DOS\PRINT.SYS LPT1=(4201,,2)
```

VDISK.SYS

Use VDISK.SYS to install a RAM disk. Step 13 describes the installation of RAM disks in detail.

RAM disks

Appendix A

The EMS Driver's Options

DR DOS comes with an EMS driver that provides LIM 4.0 expanded memory specification on computers with extended memory. The device driver EMM386.SYS (for 80386 or 80486 computers) is installed using the DEVICE command. (Warning: Take care not to use HIDEVICE!) Syntax is as follows:

```
DEVICE= EMM386.SYS [/FRAME=AUTO|NONE|nnnn]
[/KB=0|] [/AUTOSCAN start-end]
[/INCLUDE=start-end] [/VIDEO]
[/BDOS=AUTO|xxxx] [/EXCLUDE=start-end]
[/USE=start-end] [/ROM=AUTO|start-end]
```

Each of the options shown here can be abbreviated to the first letter after the slash. This appendix describes these options.

[/FRAME=xxxx]

This option controls the type of LIM 4.0 emulation. The settings shown in Table A.1 are valid.

Setting	Effect
AUTO	The EMS driver automatically scans the entire memory for a free contiguous area of 64K. This setting is the default.
NONE	Disables support for expanded memory. Use this option when you don't need expanded memory but want to use some other features of the EMS driver.
nnnn	Explicitly defines the start address of a free contiguous 64K memory area. If there is no contiguous 64K of memory available, an error message will be displayed.

Table A.1: /FRAME's settings

[/KB=*xxxx*]

This option specifies the amount of expanded memory the EMS driver is to provide. If you don't enter the option, all available memory will be used. The following values are possible for *xxxx*:

0   All available extended memory will be used for LIM memory.

nnnn   *nnnn* kilobytes of extended memory are used for LIM memory.

[/AUTOSCAN=*start-end*]

This option automatically scans the area of memory defined by *start-end* for a 64K contiguous memory area. For example, you could scan the area of memory from C000 through FFFF.

[/INCLUDE=*start-end*]

Using /INCLUDE you can define an area of memory you assume to include a free 64K of contiguous memory. /INCLUDE's most common function is to use portions of upper memory that would otherwise be ignored. You could use /AUTOSCAN instead of /INCLUDE, but it is somewhat slower due to the more thorough tests it performs.

[/EXCLUDE=*start-end*]

This option is the opposite of /INCLUDE. It defines an area of upper memory that should not be used as a window for LIM 4.0 EMS. Using /EXCLUDE lets you specifically exclude areas of memory from being checked for usability in cases where you know this would produce conflicts.

[/VIDEO]

If your computer has a MDA, Hercules, or CGA video adapter, this option allows conventional memory to be increased by 64K. It can only be used on systems with 640K of conventional memory, which the /VIDEO option then extends to 704K.

[/BDOS=*xxxx*]

This option relocates the DR DOS kernel BDOS into upper memory, thereby freeing up conventional memory for applications. /BDOS's options are shown in Table A.2.

Options	Effect
AUTO	Scans upper memory for a contiguous area of 37K and copies BDOS into it. If no free memory area is found, the segment FFFF is used instead.
FFFF	Relocates the DR DOS kernel to the segment FFFF in upper memory.
nnnn	Relocates the 37K DR DOS kernel to the address in upper memory specified by *nnnn*.

Table A.2: BDOS's options

[/USE=*start-end*]

/USE is identical to /INCLUDE, except that when /USE is specified, EMM386 memory tests are overridden and EMM386 uses the specified upper memory directly.

[/ROM=*start-end*]

This copies slow ROM into fast RAM. No additional memory is freed in process but, on the contrary, more memory is used. A

ROM copied to RAM usually works much more quickly, thus making your computer faster. To avoid conflicts, the ROM copied to conventional memory is given the same address as the original ROM.

[/ROM=AUTO]

This option copies all ROM areas it finds to RAM and in doing so improves the speed of the whole system.

Examples

In the first example, the area of memory from C000-FFFF is automatically scanned for a free area, whereby the area from E000 to EFFF is to be excluded. The system kernel should furthermore be copied to upper memory (the start address for this 64K area is determined automatically):

```
DEVICE=EMM386.SYS /F=AUTO /B=AUTO /E=E000-EFFF
```

In the following example, the memory window for LIM 4.0 is explicitly defined from address C400. Not all the extended memory should be made available as expanded memory, but only 1 Mb:

```
DEVICE=EMM386.SYS /F=C400 /KB=1024
```

Appendix B

Commands for Laptops

DR DOS is particularly well-suited for use on portable computers and provides several features geared especially to the needs of laptop users. For example, DR DOS is ROM-compatible, so the system does not have to be booted from disk. (Laptop makers can install DR DOS in ROM.) In addition, DR DOS provides special commands designed to meet the requirements of a portable computer. This appendix deals with these special commands.

CURSOR

The CURSOR command lets you set the flash rate of the cursor, which is a particularly useful capability for users of laptops with LCD screens. On LCD long-persistence displays, the cursor blinks faster than the display can handle and thus becomes difficult to locate. CURSOR can also display the cursor as a block instead of a single line to make it easier to see. CURSOR's syntax is as follows:

LCD screens

```
CURSOR [/H] [/Snn] [/C] [OFF]
```

Table B.1 summarizes CURSOR's options.

Option	Effect
/H	Displays help text.
/Snn	Specifies the cursor flash interval in units of one-twentieth of a second. Possible settings range from 1 to 20; the default is one-fifth of a second.
/C	Facilitates CGA compatibility, preventing the snow-like interference that occurs on some monitors when the cursor flashes.
OFF	Disables the software cursor and activates the hardware cursor.

Table B.1: The CURSOR command's options

To work with a block cursor that flashes four times a second, type

CURSOR /S5

FILELINK

*File
transfer
via cable*

FILELINK allows files to be transferred between two computers connected by a serial cable. This capability is most useful when it is not possible to transfer files between computers using disks. Portable computers, for example, are often not equipped with a disk drive, so that file transfer via cable is the only possible means of communication.

FILELINK needs to be installed on both systems, although the program can copy itself automatically from source to destination so long as DR DOS is installed on both computers. FILELINK operates in two different modes: *master* and *slave*.

In slave mode, FILELINK merely acts in response to requests from the computer on which it is installed as master. The requests are formulated and the responses displayed on the master computer. FILELINK's syntax is as follows:

FILELINK [/H] *command* [@] [*source*]
[*destination*] [*port*] [/A] [/D:*date*] [/H] [/M]
[/P] [/R] [/S] [/U]

Command defines one of the following commands:

DIRECTORY (DIR)

DUPLICATE (DUP)

QUIT (QUI)

RECEIVE (REC)

SETUP (SET)

SLAVE (SLA)

TRANSMIT (TRA)

Table B.2 summarizes FILELINK's options.

Option	Effect
@	*Source* defines a list of file names to be copied.
Source	Specifies the file names of the files to be copied. The files are renamed at the destination, assuming *destination* is explicitly defined.
Destination	Names the destination file names, unless the files are to retain the same name in the destination as in the source.
Port	Specifies the serial communications port and baud rate to be used.
/A	Copies only the files modified since the last BACKUP or XCOPY /M command.
/D:*date*	Copies only the files created or modified since the specified date.
/H	Copies files with the hidden or system attribute.
/M	Copies only files with archive attributes. If these files already exist at the destination, their archive attribute must be deleted there.
/P	Forces you to confirm each file before copying.
/R	Overwrites even read-only files.
/S	FILELINK copies all the files in the source's subdirectories.
/U	Copies only those files that either do not exist in the destination or else do exist there but are older than the matching files in the source.

Table B.2: The FILELINK command's options

FILELINK and Baud Rate

To save yourself having to redefine the parameters for FILELINK each time you use it, you can specify the baud rate and the communications port to be used as default values. To do this, use the SETUP command:

```
FILELINK SETUP COM1: 115200
```

First, specify the name of the device connected to the serial port, that is, COM1, COM2, or COM3. Then determine the baud rate. The rates in Table B.3 are valid.

Baud Rate	Abbreviation
115200	115
56700	56
38400	38
19200	19
9600	96
4800	48
2400	24
1200	12
600	60
300	30
150	15
110	11

Table B.3: Valid baud rates and their abbreviations

To view the current FILELINK settings, simply use the SETUP command without parameters. (FILELINK settings are also made with SETUP.) FILELINK will display its current default settings on the screen.

Transferring Data with FILELINK

FILELINK must be installed on both computers for data to be transferred between them. To copy FILELINK from the master to the slave, use the DUPLICATE command, which causes FILELINK to be copied in full to the slave and installed there. You must, of course, specify the name of the serial port and the desired baud rate:

*Copying
FILELINK*

```
FILELINK DUPLICATE COM1: 115
```

To use FILELINK, you have to put it into slave mode. If you don't explicitly enter data transmission specifications, the default values will be used:

```
FILELINK SLAVE COM1: 115
```

The master computer must also be activated. Put FILELINK on the master computer into master mode as follows:

```
FILELINK MASTER COM1: 115
```

Now, use TRANSMIT to transfer data from the master to the slave computer. Similarly, use RECEIVE to transmit data from the slave to the master computer. You can make use of FILELINK's many options to copy files:

```
FILELINK TRANSMIT *.TXT /S
FILELINK RECEIVE *.COM /H /S
```

Displaying Directories

The DIRECTORY command lets you output a directory listing from the slave computer to the master computer.

```
FILELINK DIR
```

The options summarized in Table B.4 can be used when displaying a directory:

Option	Effect
/A	Displays only files with archive attributes.
/D:*date*	Displays only files created or modified since *date*.
/H	Displays files with hidden or system attributes.
/S	Displays files in subdirectories.
/P	Displays directories a screenful at a time.

Table B.4: The DIR command's options

Finally, you conclude your work on both the slave and master computer with QUIT:

```
FILELINK QUIT
```

Index